Legal Almanac Series No. 32

CRIMES AND PENALTIES

By
Bertha R. White

Revised Edition

1970
OCEANA PUBLICATIONS, INC.
Dobbs Ferry, New York

This is a revised edition of the thirty-second number in a series of LEGAL ALMANACS which bring you the law on various subjects in nontechnical language. These books do not take the place of your attorney's advice, but they can introduce you to your legal rights and responsibilities.

(former Legal Almanac #32 - CRIMES AND PENALTIES by Theresa Berlin Stuchiner, LL.B)

Library of Congress Catalog Card Number: 74-104116

International Standard Book Number: 0-379-11066-0

Manufactured in the United States of America

For Kermit D. White

TABLE OF CONTENTS

Chapter 5

TYPICAL CRIMINAL PROCEDURE

Chapter 6

LANDMARK SUPREME COURT DECISIONS INTERPRETING
THE FOURTH, FIFTH, SIXTH, AND FOURTEENTH AMEND-
MENTS TO THE U.S. CONSTITUTION 45

INTRODUCTION

Criminal law is in essence a means of social control, and grows ever more complex in our complex society. It is as old as the murderer Cain, and as new as the most recent campus riot. Because of the multiplicity of acts of omission and commission punishable as crimes in our fifty states, it is necessary to limit the scope of this book to the major crimes, so as to give a better understanding of them.

Each of the states has its own definitions and penalties for crimes and misdemeanors, and the law varies from one to another. In addition, where the Congress has decreed that some act is a crime and has provided a penalty for it, the federal courts will try the wrongdoer, but under a Supreme Court ruling they will not try any common law crimes not enumerated in federal acts.

Our law originated in the common law of England, which goes back to the ancient times when there were unwritten laws originating in custom and usage. Gradually certain customs came to be adopted as the way to deal with a certain set of facts, either in controversies between men or in misdeeds. Judges considered themselves bound by prior similar cases, so in the later period the common law was fixed by judicial decision, and then by legislation, which restated and added to or changed the common law.

When the colonists came to the United States from England, they brought with them this body of law, statutory and common. Together with the laws enacted in England before the Revolution, this formed the basis of our law in the states, and still governs, except where changed or abolished by individual state legislatures. Louisiana is an exception to this, since it was settled by the French, who used the Civil Law system as it developed on the continent of Europe. But even Louisiana has adopted some common law principles, as may be seen in comparing her criminal statutes in the tables with those of other states.

Because of the similarity of the laws as they developed from

1

the common law basis in the fifty states, criminal laws may be discussed in a general manner, with specific references to the statutes of each state for a definition of the crime and the punishment for it.

Chapter 1

CRIMINAL ACTS IN GENERAL

Criminal law has its beginnings in the dim past, when men first began to live together in society. Its purpose is not primarily to detect and punish wrongdoers, but to define socially unacceptable actions, those which violate law and order, cause harm to another person or his property, or are detrimental to the public interest or welfare.

Modern criminal law is derived from the English common law, which recognized three types of crimes: felonies, misdemeanors, and treason, the latter not to be discussed here. Statutes have added new crimes and concepts to the basic common law felonies of murder, manslaughter, rape, sodomy, robbery, larceny, arson, and burglary. Generally felonies are crimes for which the punishment is death or imprisonment in the state prison for more than one year, with other penalties possibly being invoked, such as loss of civil and political rights, professional licenses, and so on. All crimes not felonies are termed misdemeanors.

Certain elements are necessary in order to constitute a crime. One generally says there must be the criminal intent and the criminal act or omission. Mere intent is not punished, but an attempt to commit a crime may be. Intent is provided by circumstantial or direct evidence, but it is usually inferred from the circumstantial evidence. Intent is a frame of mind that leads one to criminal conduct.

Motive differs from intent, for it is the emotional impulse which induces the act, such as hate, greed, envy, fear. Motive does not need to be shown or proven by the prosecution, but it is considered in establishing the presumption of innocence of the accused.

It is necessary to point out that certain criminal offenses

do not require showing criminal intent, such as sales of mis-branded or impure articles, violations of traffic regulations, and general police regulations for health, safety and welfare.

Criminal negligence may also make an act a crime without criminal intent, such as negligent homicide, so negligence is often an element of crime.

There must also be a criminal act or omission. The act cannot be independent of the intent. Failure to act may be punished where the person is under a duty to act, such as failing to file a tax return or an accident report.

Also required is what is known as the "corpus delicti," a legal concept which does not necessarily mean the murder victim. This concept is extended to refer to the body or elements of the crime, which consist of the fact of the injury or harm done, and the existence of a criminal cause resulting in that injury. This must be proven, not by out of court admissions or confession of the defendant, but by satisfactory evidence apart from this. It may be by circumstantial evidence.

The law considers it a sufficient criminal act where a person attempts to commit a crime but does not succeed. To constitute an attempt there must be the specific intent to commit a certain crime and a direct but unsuccessful act done toward its commission. The act must be such that the crime would have been accomplished were it not for an interruption. In attempting the crime, a person may complete another one, such as murder during an attempted burglary, in which case he will be punished for the crime committed.

It is also considered a criminal act when a person solicits another to commit a specific crime, even though the person may not do so. Urging or inciting is a sufficient criminal act, even if the second party does not do the act. In some states soliciting a person to commit even a misdemeanor is considered a crime.

A conspiracy is an agreement between two or more persons to do an unlawful act, or to accomplish a lawful act through unlawful means. One or more of the parties is to do the overt act. Thus, a conspiracy is a criminal partnership. The mere unlawful agreement is enough to constitute the crime, however, without commission of the act. Usually in criminal law an unlawful intent is not of itself punished unless it is followed by an act which constitutes the crime or an attempt. It is reasoned that punishing conspiracy as a felony is wise because criminal activities of people acting together are so much more dangerous and more likely to succeed than the intent of an individual acting alone. Each member of a conspiracy is liable for the acts of any of them in carrying out the general aim of the conspiracy--all acts, in other words, that are the reasonable and probable consequences of the common unlawful conspiracy.

Often when a crime is committed, more than one person is involved. The law does not treat equally the various parties to a crime, except in the case of misdemeanors. At common law there are principals in the first degree, who actually commit the crime, and principals in the second degree, for example those present and aiding and abetting in the commission of the crime. The phrase "aid and abet" is often misunderstood. Usually to be liable as an abetter the defendant must have instigated or advised the crime or have been present when it was committed in order to assist. To be guilty he must have taken part in its planning and have taken affirmative action in its commission.

There is usually no difference in the punishment given first and second degree principals. If the crime is the result of two or more required acts, all guilty parties who perform any of these acts are joint principals in the first degree. An illustration of this is where some members of a counterfeiting gang may obtain the paper and ink, another may engrave the plates, and others may pass the money. One does not need to be present at all of these times in order to be a principal.

A principal in the second degree is one who did not do the criminal act himself or with the aid of an innocent agent (like a nurse who unknowingly administers poison to a patient), but is guilty of the felony because of having assisted, advised, ordered or encouraged the crime, whether he was actually or constructively present at the time. If he is absent at the time of commission, he is an accessory before the fact instead. Or he may be what is called constructively present, such as being a lookout at a bank robbery. In other words, he is cooperating with the criminals who are committing the crime, in a position to help them if necessary and to aid in the success of the crime.

Accessories may be accessories before the fact or accessories after the fact, the first being those who may advise about commission of the crime, procure someone to help commit

5

it, and the latter those who after the crime may hide a principal or assist him in escaping. Some states have abolished the differences in punishment as to the parties to the crime, and punish all principals equally with accessories before the fact, except for the one who is the prosecution witness. Since the accessory before the fact is not present physically when the crime is committed, he cannot give aid at that moment, but may have assisted even a long time ago. He may simply suggest victims or make general plans for crimes. An accessory after the fact, knowing of the criminal's guilt, gives aid in an effort to prevent his discovery, arrest, trial, or punishment. The aid given must be of a type that tends to frustrate the course of justice. Unlike the accessory before the fact, the accessory after the fact may be present when the crime is committed.

Chapter 2

OFFENSES OR CRIMES AGAINST THE PERSON

HOMICIDE

Homicide is the killing by one human being of another human being. Not every killing is a crime. Common and statutory law usually distinguish between these types of homicide: criminal homicide, murder, manslaughter, second-degree murder, voluntary and involuntary homicide, and justifiable homicide.

The reason for this classification was to divide criminal from non-criminal homicide and to distinguish between the crimes when capital punishment is the penalty and those where it is not. The various states in the United States have made their own distinctions, which will be apparent in the statutory tables in Appendix I.

To constitute homicide, a human being must be killed by another human being. If a man kills an animal, or an animal kills a man, there is no homicide. However, an animal could be the means of doing the killing, such as would be the case if a man loosed a wild animal upon someone. Also, in most states, for the law to recognize homicide, the person must die within a year and a day from the time the act alleged to have caused the death occurred.

The death does not need to have been caused by a positive act, but can be because of an omission or a failure to act where a person is under a legal duty to act, as in a father's failure to provide adequately for his children. But the criminal act must be the proximate cause without intervening causes.

Where there is no intervening factor, the defendant is guilty if death results from his act or omission. If arson results in the death of a person who tries to put out the fire, the arsonist is guilty of murder. Homicide occurring during a robbery is murder. It is not necessary to prove anything but the intent to commit robbery. This common law "felony-murder" rule is sometimes modified if the statutory definition includes the word "purposely" as part of the definition of murder.

If a defendant robs a victim and leaves him lying in the street where he is run over by an automobile, is it murder? This is where an independent force comes in. The rule applied here is that the defendant should reasonably have foreseen that an automobile might have run over his victim. If the intervening cause is foreseeable, the defendant is responsible.

An unborn child at common law could not be the subject of homicide. An injury to a pregnant woman, causing the child to be born dead, was not himicide. For it to be murder or manslaughter the child must be born alive and then later die of the prenatal injuries it received. This is still generally the rule.

MURDER

Murder at common law was defined as the unlawful killing of a human being with malice aforethought. Many of the state laws incorporate this into their definition of murder at the present time. There are two kinds of malice, express and implied. Express is where there is actual intent to kill the person killed. On the other hand implied malice is where there is an intent to inflict great bodily harm, or where an act is done willfully which has the tendency to cause death or great bodily harm, or where a homicide is committed during the course of some other felony.

Malice is a state of mind where one does not care what consequences of his act develop as far as causing death or great harm. There is a wanton disregard of the probable harm one's conduct may cause, or the actual intent to cause harm. A sniper taking shots at cars on a freeway is acting in this manner.

At common law there were no degrees for murder, and the punishment was death. While our state statutes have modified and changed the common law definition for murder, most of them base it upon the intent to cause the death with deliberation and premeditation. Many of our states have adopted the idea of two degrees of murder, partly in an initial attempt to limit the death penalty. The Commonwealth of Pennsylvania was the first

8

to define the two degrees of murder, and punish only the first with death. The preamble to the Pennsylvania statute indicates that its primary purpose was to limit the death penalty to the most depraved murderers: "The punishment of death ought never to be inflicted where it is not absolutely necessary to the public safety." Ths most common definition of murder is taken from this Pennsylvania Act of 1794. It defines first degree murder as "all murder which shall be perpetrated by means of poison, or by lying in wait, or by any other kind of willful, deliberate and premeditated killing," and "homicides occurring in the course of the commission or attempt to commit arson, rape, robbery or burglary," the so-called "felony-murder" rule. Approximately one-half of the states follow this definition in varying language. A comparison of the summaries for murder and manslaughter in the appendix will show the different technical definitions used.

The words "deliberation" and "premeditation" as used in these statutes, have also been given technical definitions by the courts. "Deliberation" implies a decision made calmly, with the reasons for and against being examined and weighed, before embarking on a course of action. "Premeditation" implies a previous plan or design for action. In some states the two words are used as synonyms; elsewhere "deliberation" implies reflection, no matter how brief, upon the act before its commission, as distinguished from sudden impulse; while "premeditation" implies a previous design which might include acts on impulse.

Benjamin Cardozo, the famous Supreme Court justice and legal philosopher, felt that one reason behind this describing of the words was a way of allowing a jury "to find the lesser degrees of murder when the suddenness of the intent, the vehemence of the passion seems to call irresistibly for the exercise of mercy."*

Another noticeable similarity in the statutes of several states is the inclusion in the definition of first-degree murder of homicides unintentionally committed by an act greatly dangerous to the lives of others, indicating a depraved mind regardless of human life. The courts generally limit the application of this part of the law to cases where the lives of many people have been en-

---

*"What Medicine can do for Law," Law and Literature, 100-101 (1930).

dangered by some action. Premeditation and deliberation may be inferred from the circumstances surrounding the killing, such as threats made by the defendant in the past, the kind of weapon used, actions after the murder, such as trying to conceal it, etc. Of course the defendant may offer evidence to show his mental state, that he was insane, intoxicated, incapable of premeditating or of malice aforethought. If lying in wait can be shown, no other proof of premeditation is necessary. Here generally the killer must be concealed in ambush.

FELONY-MURDER

In some states the definition of first degree murder includes homicides committed during the perpetration of another felony. This is the felony-murder rule, which is the doctrine that makes it murder to kill a person, innocent bystander or anyone, during the commission of another felony, usually burglary, arson, rape, or robbery. The killing does not need to be intentional, and premeditation and malice are not necessary. The only criminal intent needed is the specific intent to commit a particular felony, the elements of which must be proven. A not unusual example of this is where a rape victim is murdered, or where an innocent bystander is shot by a fleeing robber. The rule has been applied also to cases where one co-conspirator shot another. Certain limits have been placed on this felony-murder rule. For example, in New York the felony must be independent of the homicide or it cannot be a basis for conviction. In California the only requirement is that there must be specific intent to commit the felony, such as burglary, mayhem, robbery. As long as the felony and the murder are parts of a continuous transaction, and the elements of the felony are proven, the felony-murder rule will be followed in that state.

Some state statutes have gone beyond the common law rule by declaring that the commission of any involuntary killing during the course of any unlawful act tending to destroy life is murder. Under Georgia law it was murder for a motorist to kill a pedestrian when he was driving while intoxicated at an excessive speed on the wrong side of the road.

Other states have restricted the felony-murder rule where they do not consider the statutory felony sufficiently dangerous for the application of the rule. In Michigan, where the sale of liquor was a statutory felony, a seller was found not guilty of the death of a customer who died of alcoholism and exposure to the cold. In Pennsylvania it was held that it was not first degree murder where death resulted from felonious statutory rape.

SECOND DEGREE MURDER

Most states having degrees of murder define second degree murder as all other kinds of homicide which would have been murder at common law. Some define it as murder committed purposely and maliciously but without deliberation and premeditation. In other states homicides evincing a "depraved and malignant heart," as one example, are designated as second degree murder. As was said before, the primary purpose for dividing murder into degrees was to limit the severest punishment to the most serious offenses. The death penalty is not imposed for murder in the second degree.

At times an unlawful killing is found to be second degree murder at the end of a trial because neither side proved it to be something else. The prosecution may prove the elements (corpus delicti) of homicide, but is not able to prove premeditation or sufficient provocation and heat of passion. With this evidence, malice aforethought is legally presumed, and the proper verdict is second degree murder.

MANSLAUGHTER

The crimes of murder and manslaughter constitute just one offense under the early common law of England. Before the laws on the subject, any killing was punishable by death and forfeit of land and other property, but the crime was within benefit of clergy* where the life of the criminal could be saved if he qualified. Then the more serious type of homicide, murder with mal-

---

*At first only clergy were entitled to this "benefit," but the courts extended it to all who could read, on the legal fiction that if a person could read, he must be a member of the clergy.

ice aforethought, was removed from benefit of clergy, the word murder was applied to homicide with malice aforethought, and the term manslaughter was invented for the other lesser crime.

Some of the states, as may be seen upon consulting the chart, have subdivided either or both murder and manslaughter into different degrees. As stated before, murder is distinguished from manslaughter in that it is a homicide that is willful, deliberate or premeditated, committed with malice aforethought, or committed while engaged in perpetrating, or attempting to perpetrate, some other felony. On the other hand manslaughter will be the crime charged if the provocation is sufficient, such that it would cause a person to act from passion rather than from reason. Insulting words or actions alone are not considered sufficient provocation to reduce a killing from murder to manslaughter, even though some other slight additional act may do so, or may determine the punishment if more than one penalty is allowed by law. The circumstances here are such that the state of mind of the one doing the killing must not be malicious, and he has not actually premeditated the killing as, for example, killing someone in a sudden and angry fist fight, being suddenly and forcefully assaulted, or finding one's wife or husband in an adulterous act. The provocation must be related to the sudden angry passion, and the killing must follow the provocation before the heat of passion cools.

How long a time comprises this cooling-off period depends upon whether, in the time since the provocation was received, the mind of the ordinary reasonable man would have cooled and calmed sufficiently that he would again be acting by reason, not emotion. The test is whether, considering all the circumstances, the provocation and the condition of the accused, a reasonable man under like circumstances would calm himself in that period of time between the provocative act and the killing, or whether, after a lapse of time, he could again become so emotionally stirred and provoked, that he would relive the provocative act and be aroused to sufficient passion to kill without reason or reflection.

A person may kill after a long time during which he has been continually provoked but has controlled his temper time after time, until the final emotional outburst. Passion may also be revived by being brought again to the person's mind after a cooling period, so that he is controlled by that feeling, as where one is confronted by his mother's murderer, and may become provoked enough to lose control and kill.

Some state statutes have divided manslaughter into voluntary, discussed above, which is intentional homicide, and involuntary, unintentional, excusable or negligent homicide, or manslaughter first and second degree. A comparison of the state laws regarding manslaughter reveals that a number distinguish between voluntary and involuntary manslaughter in practically the same terms as the common law. The maximum penalty for voluntary manslaughter is more severe than that for involuntary manslaughter. Some states have followed the New York Penal Code in defining first degree manslaughter as acting with intent to cause serious physical injury and causing death instead, or intending to cause death but doing it under circumstances which do not constitute murder first degree because done under influence of extreme emotional disturbance. Usually then second degree manslaughter is defined as homicide caused by one acting in such a manner as to recklessly cause death but without the intent to do so. Some states define manslaughter simply as unlawfully killing a person, sometimes adding the words without malice and without deliberation, and provide only one penalty. A number of states do not define the crime, but give the penalty. It is interesting to note that sometimes there is a provision for payment of a heavy monetary penalty in addition to, or instead of, a prison sentence, particularly for second degree manslaughter.

NEGLIGENT HOMICIDE

Just as the line between murder and manslaughter is a shadowy one, so is the line between manslaughter and non-criminal or civil negligence. A homicide resulting from an act unduly dangerous to life or limb may be manslaughter, murder, or civil negligence. Usually the difference between the negligence which is deemed civil wrong and that which is criminal is based on words such as wanton, reckless, gross, or culpable, as distinguished from simple or ordinary negligence. The degree of the risk is usually the difference between civil and criminal negligence.

Negligent action causing death is action which falls below the usual standard of care observed by the ordinary prudent man and established by law to protect lives from unreasonable risk of danger. Whoever causes harm as a result of negligence incurs liability. If it is simple negligence, the one harmed would have the right to receive damages; if criminal negligence, the actor is guilty of a criminal offense when his standard of care does not measure up to that of a responsible person. Criminal negligence is usually characterized by reckless conduct. If the act causing death is merely forbidden by law and not otherwise wrong, the death resulting is excusable if not willful or the result of criminal negligence. However, a death resulting from intentional violation of a law resulting from the desire to protect human life, such as an anti-riot law, would be criminal negligence.

JUSTIFIABLE AND EXCUSABLE HOMICIDE

Justifiable and excusable homicides are sometimes termed innocent homicide, in that they do not involve criminal guilt and no blame is attached. Situations arise in everyday life that come within the category of innocent homicide. If commanded by law the homicide is justifiable and therefore not punishable. One example is killing an enemy in battle in wartime, and another is executing a death sentence upon a convicted criminal, one who has committed a capital offense. Homicides authorized by law also include the killing of a criminal in self-defense when the one doing the killing is in imminent danger of death or great bodily harm, and is not himself at fault, the killing of a murderer if necessary in arresting him or in preventing his escape, or killing him if there is great resistance, when a criminal is engaged in committing a felony with great force, such as rape or robbery.

Not all felonies are such as would justify assault or homicide in order to prevent them. A felony that is not accompanied by violence or surprise does not require homicide or force to prevent it. For example, the prevention of the crime of larceny would not justify a homicide. Nor would homicide be justified if done to prevent simple assault and battery, which does not endanger life or threaten great bodily harm.

Homicide which is not commanded or authorized by law is excusable if it is committed under a situation where no criminal guilt is involved. Where one boxer kills another in a state where boxing is legal, the death would be excusable. In a situation where someone is lawfully shooting at a target and without negligence

14

kills someone, that is also excusable, because accidental.

Homicide occurring while a person is defending himself may be either justifiable or excusable.* If it occurs during a fight, and self-defense is claimed, the party who was threatened must in some states show that he had retreated as far as possible before taking his opponent's life. The one committing the homicide must believe that his own life is in imminent danger. However, where a person is assaulted in his own home, there is no requirement that he must first retreat. In every case of self-defense the person who kills must not have provoked the fight nor have been the aggressor. Here the homicide is justifiable.

If a practical joke is played upon a person by someone who is a very convincing actor and seems to be a genuine menace, but has a fake weapon, the person threatened may really feel that his life is in danger and kill to protect it. The homicide is here not justifiable, but is excusable because of the mistake of fact. Or if a person is grievously assaulted and attacked, so that killing his assailant is justifiable, but he mistakenly shoots an innocent bystander instead, the homicide is excusable, since the shot was fired without criminal negligence.

CRIMINAL RESPONSIBILITY

Homicides committed by those who are irresponsible are not punished as criminal homicides, even though they are still considered criminal acts. Among those who are considered irresponsible are children, the drunk, and the insane. Under common law children under the age of seven years were presumed incapable of harboring criminal intent and so were not criminally responsible for their actions. In some states the age has been raised to ten years. From seven to fourteen years the common law presumed children incapable of forming criminal intent, but this presumption could be rebutted by showing that the particular child had sufficient intelligence to distinguish between right and wrong. After a child reached the age of fourteen it was presumed that he could form criminal intent, but this presumption could

---

*For a discussion of self-defense, see Baum, "Law of Self-Defense," Legal Almanac No. 64 (1970).

also be rebutted by the accused.

Usually a man who is insane is not criminally responsible for his acts, because he is considered to be incapable of forming a criminal intent. The courts vary as to the test of insanity, but the usual rule is whether the person is capable of distinguishing between right and wrong. This is called the rule of M'Naghten's case. Daniel M'Naghten killed the secretary to the Prime Minister of England, Robert Peel, thinking he was shooting Peel. He was acquitted of the murder on the ground of insanity because of the jury instruction that the defendant should be convicted if he was in a sound state of mind, or acquitted if he did not have the "use of his understanding so as to know he was doing a wrong and wicked act." This 1843 case may be read in Volume Eight of the English reports on page 718. Because of the fact that the intended victim was Prime Minister, the House of Lords after debate asked certain questions of the judges. Their answers were printed with the report of the case, and for this reason the case took on great importance.

Under this rule it must be proven that the accused was under such a defect of reason from disease of the mind that he did not know the nature or quality of the act he was committing, or if he did know, then he did not know that he was doing wrong. The law in this case had been developing in England for centuries, and was thus set by this ruling. In about half of the states this right-wrong test was made the determining factor of criminal incapacity because of a mental disorder, but in the past fifteen years has been modified.

When a homicide is committed by an insane person who has some sane intervals, then it must be determined whether he was sane or insane at the time of the act. His condition at the time of the act determines whether or not he is responsible, but his behavior before and after is considered to determine his condition at the time of the crime.

In some instances drunkenness affects a person's responsibility for a homicide. At common law it was no defense to murder, no matter how excessive, and did not excuse or lessen the offense. Even though the person was temporarily deprived of his reason, he was as responsible as a sober person. Intoxication and insanity are not on the same level as far as responsibility or criminal capacity is concerned, because intoxication is usually voluntarily contracted, whether it is intoxication from alcohol or from drugs. In states where there are different degrees of murder, and an actual intent to kill, or deliberation or premeditation, is necessary for murder first degree, but not for second degree, drunkenness may be shown to establish the absence of intent needed for a verdict of murder first degree. However, it would not be a defense to a charge of murder second degree where actual intent and premeditation are not required.

If a person is not voluntarily intoxicated, but is so because of the fraudulent scheme of another, and does not realize what he is drinking, or has been forced to drink, criminal incapacity to form intent is not necessarily established. The only sure fact is that the person's behavior is without blame and so is to be dealt with in the same way as if caused by mental disease or a mental defect. Then the person could be shown to have been in such a state of mind that he was incapable of acting with the deliberation and premeditation necessary by law for murder in the first degree. This is not the same as if a person has formed an intent to commit homicide and then had become drunk to strengthen his nerve.

ASSAULT AND BATTERY

At common law assault and battery were considered misdemeanors, though serious ones could be charged as attempts to commit the intended crime, such as murder, rape, etc. At present in some states there is what is termed aggravated assault, such as assault to do great bodily harm, with intent to rape or rob, for example, or assault with a deadly weapon. In others there are degrees of assault and battery, depending upon how serious the offense is. The greater the seriousness, the greater the punishment.

An assault is an unlawful attempt to commit a battery upon the person of another. A battery is intentional unlawful use of force upon another person. One can have assault without battery, that is, the unsuccessful attempt. The most usual examples of assault and battery are hitting another with a fist, a stick or stone, knifing, or shooting. Inducing a person to take poison, or throwing lye upon him, or exposing a child or an adult to bad weather, all constitute assault and battery, though no physical

17

force is applied directly to the victim.

For the crime to be assault and battery, there must be more than the mere intent to commit a battery or injury. The element of attempt must be shown, that is, a specific intent to commit, coupled with an act that is close to accomplishment and not merely preparation.

In California and a few other states, the person must have the present ability to commit the crime. A threat with an unloaded gun is no crime.* While a threat is not enough, there may be difficulty in distinguishing between a threat and the assault. Getting a weapon ready without attempting to use it, or without the ability to use it at the time, probably would not constitute an assault. If someone says, "If you weren't my brother-in-law, I would beat you within an inch of your life," it would not be an assault as there is no intent, but merely a threat without intent to commit injury.

Sometimes an unlawful act causing an injury, although done unintentionally, will be considered a battery instead of an accident. If the act is a crime, and malum in se (wrong in itself), and the injury is the natural result of the act, there may be an assault and battery. For example, aiming and shooting a gun into a crowd and hitting someone is assault and battery, or murder or manslaughter if a person is killed. If the act is malum prohibitum (a prohibited wrong), an act which is not inherently evil or immoral, but is forbidden by law, such as driving in excess of the speed limit, the driver will not be guilty of assault and battery if he injures someone, but will be civilly responsible. The case might be assault and battery if the person is guilty of gross negligence, such as driving while drunk on the wrong side of a freeway.

It is important to note in connection with assault and battery that great force is not necessary to constitute the crime. Even a touching, both in tort and criminal law, may be sufficient. A degree of force may be enough without any pain or bruising, as, for example, when a man caresses and fondles a woman without her consent, even though he is not overwhelming

---

*However, in many states, including California, it is a misdemeanor to display a loaded or unloaded gun in a threatening manner.

her with violence.

AGGRAVATED ASSAULT

In most of the states there are laws dealing with felonious assaults and batteries, or what we might call aggravated assault or assault with intent to murder, rob, rape, or do great bodily harm. These crimes would be punished as felonies. To prove aggravated assault it is necessary to show the specific intent to commit the crime of murder, rape, or whatever it is. Specific intent, not apparent intent, is necessary and is usually proved by circumstantial evidence.* There must be more than preparation or a threat of harm at some future time, but pointing a loaded gun is usually an assault. Assault with a deadly weapon is usually punished as aggravated assault.

A deadly weapon is one which is likely to cause death if used in the customary manner. The courts usually take note that loaded guns, axes, hammers, etc., are deadly weapons, but leave it up to the jury to decide whether other weapons are deadly within the circumstances of the case. This would include objects like a glass, a stick or a stone.

An assault with intent to commit a particular felony differs from an attempt. For example, a defendant may commit an attempt to commit murder even though he has not yet come close enough to aim or to threaten the person, but an assault would require him to come closer. An attempt may not include an assault, but an assault clearly includes an attempt.

No injury is necessary for a person to be charged with the crime of assault with a deadly weapon. The person's aim may be diverted, so that the person is not shot, but the assault and the intent are there.

A not infrequent method in injuring, or attempting to injure, a person today is by throwing vitriol, a corrosive acid, or a chemical of some kind with the intent to injure or disfigure the person. This is of course a felony, requiring a specific intent and also usually a showing that some of the acid, however small the quantity, touched the person, and that the act was done willfully and maliciously.

_____

*In California specific intent is not required.

Assault with intent to rape as a crime requires the intent to have intercourse against the woman's will. If the man abandons his attempt, he is guilty only of simple battery.

MAYHEM

The crime of mayhem, an aggravated battery, is defined as disfiguring or maiming a person by depriving him of a part of his body, such as an eye, a limb, an ear, or making it useless. A specific intent to maim or disfigure is not usually necessary, as malice is inferred.

RAPE

Rape is sexual intercourse with a female not the wife of the perpetrator, accomplished without her consent, by force or against her will. Usually only the slightest penetration is necessary.

If the woman is incapable of consenting because of mental condition, immaturity, or because her resistance is overcome by force or fear of harm or a drugged or intoxicated state, the law presumes that there is no consent. Consent obtained by fraud in a pretend marriage, upon pretext of medical treatment, etc., is not true consent. Likewise if someone impersonates the woman's husband, she does not in actuality consent to an act of adultery.

A husband can be guilty of aiding and abetting a third person of raping his wife, or a woman may likewise be guilty of aiding and abetting the rape of another woman. A woman of unchaste character may also be raped.

Present-day cases do not require resistance to the uttermost, where a woman is intimidated either by express or implied threats of great bodily harm. All of the force necessary to achieve intercourse and resistance to prevent it is required to prove the crime, unless the victim is under the age of consent, when the completed crime would be statutory rape. The term statutory rape is not always found in the statute books, but is generally implied to an act of intercourse with a minor, unless she is defendant's wife. Even though no resistance may be offered, or consent is given in such a case, rape is charged as it is presumed that consent cannot be given because of the extreme youth of the female. In view of the sexual revolution today, punishment for this crime may seem unduly harsh.

KIDNAPING

As common law kidnaping was a misdemeanor, but under the laws of the states it has been made a felony. When a person is held for ransom, it is treated as a capital offense.

The Lindbergh law and the federal authorities come into the picture when a kidnaped person is taken from one state to another if held for ransom or reward, and the punishment may be death unless the person is freed unharmed. After a person has been kidnaped and held for seven days there is a presumption that he has been taken across state lines, but this presumption is not conclusive.

Asportation, or carrying the person away, is essential to the crime, but the courts have interpreted the carrying away to include such varied acts as moving a person a few feet, locking bank cashiers in a vault, and jumping into a car and ordering the driver at gunpoint to take the defendant elsewhere.

Secrecy is not always essential to proving the crime, although some states have substituted for the asportation an intent to confine the victim somewhere in secret. Taking a person and keeping him against his will is false imprisonment; to seize him unlawfully and keep him in secret is kidnaping.

Chapter 3

OFFENSES AGAINST PROPERTY

THEFT AND LARCENY

At common law there were legalistic differences between the crimes of appropriation of another's property: larceny, the taking by trespass--embezzlement, misappropriation of funds by a trustee or fiduciary--and false pretenses, the obtaining of property by false representations. These terms did not serve any useful purpose, and in a number of states, such as California, these crimes were combined in the Penal Code into theft, whereas in other states, such as New York, all three were combined under the name larceny.

The purpose of combining these crimes was to avoid specifying in the indictment charging theft whether the crime is embezzlement, larceny or false pretenses, and thus avoiding the technical difficulties in pleading and proof required by the common law. However, these common law differences still exist in substance even where they have been abolished in form.

Larceny is the taking by trespass and carrying away of any personal property of another of at least nominal value, with intent to steal it. At English common law it was one of the few felonies, but under the laws of the United States it may be either a felony or a misdemeanor depending upon the value of the property that has been stolen. Under common law the thing taken had to be personal property, but statutory law has extended this to include severing and carrying away things in the nature of real property, trees, crops, etc., which are capable of being carried away.

The things taken must be capable of ownership. Taking an abandoned property or treasure trove cannot be larceny, for the real owner has given up possession and title. Wild animals are not property. Water, oil, gas and electricity are considered property after they have been confined in pipes, reservoirs, etc., and reduced to possession in some way. If they can be appropriated by someone not their owner, they can be the subject of larceny.

Under the law of larceny we consider who has possession of the article, not the title; a person may be the rightful possessor, such as a bailee, without having title. The one holding title may be guilty of larceny if he removes an automobile from a garage without paying a repair bill thereon. Also, it can be larceny to steal an article from the possession of a thief although the article was acquired and reduced to possession illegally. Here one must distinguish between possession, custody and title. A person shopping in a store may be guilty of larceny if he takes from the store, without intending to pay for it, an object turned over to him for examination, because he has custody only. However, he may have the same article delivered to his home by the store without intending to pay for it and not be guilty of larceny because the delivery to his home transferred possession to him. The driver of the delivery truck has custody of the article only. If the person pays for the goods by worthless check, it could also be larceny.

It is not larceny to take one's property from someone who has no right to hold it. If you sell furniture to someone who takes it and some other articles from your home, it is not larceny to take back the things not sold to him while he is loading them on his truck.

The taking of possession of an article is not sufficient for larceny unless the taking is by trespass, that is, without the consent of the owner. If the consent has not been obtained through trickery or force, there is no larceny, however. Leaving an article carelessly lying somewhere does not mean that consent to taking it is given. This is a technical trespass, and does not refer to trespass on real estate.

The manner of the taking is irrelevant. The property may be carried away by the actual thief in his hands, or it may be taken by tapping an electric conduit and consuming it without passing it through a meter. Or the property may be taken by an innocent person, as a young child or an insane person, who does not know the facts. Or a person may have an innocent go-

23

between deliver property to him, as when he steals a trunk by changing baggage checks at a railroad station and having the case wrongfully delivered to him. But if the property is taken from the owner through violence or by putting him in fear of trouble, the offense is not larceny but robbery.

Taking "sufficient for larceny" means that at some moment the thief must have complete independent and absolute possession and control of the thing taken. If he merely puts his hand on a woman's purse in a shopping cart but does not take it into his hand, it would not be larceny. Or if he touches a pen attached to a chain in a library, but does not break the chain, it is not larceny. The possession may be merely momentary, and the length of time the taker holds the article does not matter, if there is a sufficient carrying away of the article to meet the requirement of the crime. If the article has been segregated or moved slightly from its original position, but not from the premises, it may be a sufficient carrying away, such as where goods are concealed under a person's clothing, but he is apprehended before he can leave the building.

Larceny of an animal can be accomplished by bringing it under the thief's control and only slightly carrying it away, placing it in a pen or container. Chasing it without catching it would not be larceny. Killing cattle is not larceny unless the defendant takes possession of the hide or body and carries it away, unless the taking away has been eliminated by the statute of the particular state where the crime was committed. Altering or removing a brand from cattle with an intent to steal them might be considered larceny even in a state which had a requirement of carrying away as an element of the crime.

The time of day or night is not a material element in deciding whether or not the crime has been committed, although it may affect the seriousness of the offense if the statute divides larceny into degrees and makes it a more serious offense when occurring at nighttime. The place is also immaterial; it may be a store, dwelling, car, warehouse, or the person of the owner. Taking from the person of the owner makes it a more serious offense in some states.

An essential element of the crime of larceny is wrongful intent, intent to steal or some knowledge that the act is wrongful. Borrowing or taking by mistake is not larceny, nor is it where one

24

acts on good faith that he has permission from the true owner. If the article is taken with an intent to buy, or under good faith claim or right, it is not larceny, even though the claim may be based upon a misconception of law. An example of this is a taking by a creditor of property to satisfy his debt, where he is honestly mistaken that he has the right to be paid.

Another essential element is appropriation or deprivation of the owner. There must be intent to deprive the owner permanently of his property and an intent to appropriate it to the taker's use or to a use inconsistent with the right of the person from whom the article is taken. If there is no statute to the contrary, it is not larceny to borrow an automobile or bicycle without permission, since the taker does not intend to deprive the owner permanently of his possession.

The crime of "joy-riding" deserves special mention. It was more prevalent before automobiles were so numerous, perhaps, and there was great temptation on the part of young boys in particular to drive a car without the consent of the owner. Since these automobiles were taken with the intent to use them for a short time only, and then return them to the owners, the crime of larceny could not be charged without special statutes. Therefore the laws provided a penalty for this taking without intent to steal, making it a felony because of the damage that often resulted to the car, its high cost, and also because in larceny of motor vehicles it was difficult to secure a conviction because the thief could claim he did not intend to keep the car.

A more or less common occurrence is when the intent to appropriate to the taker's use occurs after the taking, if the original taking was without the consent of the owner or through fraud. If the defendant cannot form an intent at the time of taking because he is intoxicated, but forms the intent to convert the property to his own use when he becomes sober, then he has committed larceny. If a person is overpaid innocently, and after discovering the error uses the money for himself, he would not be guilty of larceny, but if he receives the overpayment knowingly with an intent at that time to use the excess, he would be guilty of larceny. His possession may be lawful if he acquires the goods by fraud or deceit, but if he does so with an intent to steal, it would be larceny. If he receives the goods for a particular purpose but then converts it to some other use, it is larceny if at the time he receives the article he has the intent to appropriate it for himself.

Generally, if the owner delivers property intending to give possession and title, the person taking it would not be guilty of larceny in receiving it, even though he induced delivery through fraud. He would then be guilty of the crime of false pretenses, discussed below. However, in some states this is still larceny if the title does not pass until certain conditions are met.

DEGREES OF LARCENY

The Statute of Westminster in England in 1275 classified larceny as either grand or petit (now petty), the former being a felony and a capital offense, the latter punishable by loss of goods and whipping. The classification depended upon the value of the goods stolen. Modern statutes usually retain this classification, and the amount varies between $50 and $200 as the dividing line between the two types of larceny, with the theft of some specifically named articles being automatically grand larceny. In California, for example, for a grand theft charge personal property must be of the value of $200; citrus fruits, avocadoes, olives, nuts, and artichokes of the value of $50.

The object stolen must have some legally recognized value. In California, where a lottery was illegal, a winning lottery ticket was not considered a thing of value. If there is no provision in the law for determining value, the rule is the market value of the thing stolen at that time and place. If there is no market value, it is the worth considering all the facts and circumstances in evidence. State statutes usually provide in the case of a stolen note that the value is the amount of money due and collectible on it, or in the case of books or bonds the market value, not the face value. The value of electricity or gas stolen from the owner is the price at which it is sold to the public. If property owned by the federal government is stolen, the crime is a felony if the value is over $100, or a misdemeanor if the value is less. This law also states that value is par, face, market value, or cost price, wholesale or retail, whichever is the greater sum.

Some states provide more severe penalties for larceny from dwelling houses, or from certain other places such as railcars, boats, and trailers.

FALSE PRETENSES

The crime of false pretenses actually means the crime of obtaining property by false pretenses, and was created by statute to fill a gap in the law of larceny, to which it is closely related. This occurred first in England in the time of the colonization of the New World, so was generally accepted in our common law. The new law was necessary because one requirement of the crime of larceny is that the property must be taken without the consent of the owner, and so did not cover cases where the owner was passing title to the property as well as possession, when induced to do so by fraud or deception.

Our states have enacted special statutes and have gone beyond the original law, making it a crime to obtain money, intangible personal property, deeds to real property, executing a check with knowledge that the drawer has insufficient funds, etc. In California the law even includes labor or services where employees are hired without their being advised of labor claims and judgments the employer has been unable to meet.

The elements of the crime of false pretenses are that there must be an intent to defraud, misrepresentation of a present or past fact, and actual reliance by the owner on the defendant's representation. In addition there must be an actual defrauding or the obtaining of something of value without compensation, before the person can be charged with the crime.

Intent to cheat is usually regarded as essential, but it is the intent to defraud, not the intent to receive benefit or advantage from the cheat, that is important. For example, in Texas the law specifically states that where there is a willful intent to receive a benefit or cause an injury, it is of no account that the benefit or injury does not result.

The false representation must be of a past or present fact, not something to take place in the future, and may be implied from the conduct of the defendant, such as hiding something or not disclosing it when there is a duty to speak, or it may be made expressly. A promise without a representation of an existing fact is not sufficient in the absence of a law making it so. Mere "puffing," the usual salesman's talk, is not misrepresentation,

27

upon the theory that a certain amount of it is customary and expected. Predictions of future profits are not a misrepresentation. False promises are made by false pretenses by law, and the prosecution must show the fraudulent intent, not merely that the promises have not been fulfilled. Opinions, if they are understood to be only opinions, are not false pretenses.

Examples of false representations that are frequently made are as to ownership of property, the kind or quality or condition of property, the assets of a business, credit, financial position, bills that have been paid, fake cancer cures, and the like.

The test the court uses in determining what the crime is is not whether the false pretenses would deceive an ordinary reasonable man, but whether or not the particular man who gave up his money or property was deceived. In this way the law protects those with little business sense, the gullible and the foolish.

The owner of the property must turn it over in reliance upon the false pretenses, or there is no crime. If the owner has made independent investigation as to the deal, and acts upon his findings, there is likewise no crime any more than there would be if the owner knows or believes the pretense to be false If the pretense is made later, after the property is obtained, then the crime has not been committed either. In other words, there must be a connection between the transfer of the property and the false representation. The representation may be looked upon as continuing, where there is a time between the representation and the transfer, but the representation must be before.

The pretense may be oral or written, by act or word. Some states require that it be written. In some states where a fact is not disclosed by someone bound to reveal it, that is considered a false pretense. Thus, silence may be the false representation when one is under a duty to speak.

It is interesting to note that the defendant cannot usually bring up the defense that he has given something of value in exchange for the other property. If a person is defrauded he did not get what he contracted for, even though he may not have suffered a net financial loss. If he recovers the property, he has still been the victim of the crime.

Giving a worthless check with the knowledge that there are insufficient funds to cover the check is generally considered a false pretense, but some of the states have special statutes to cover this "cheating by check." The theory on which this is based is that the drawer of the check obtains money by means of the check, and represents by writing it that he has funds in the bank sufficient to cover it. But the person who has given something of value for the check has the right to believe that there are funds in the bank, so that he will be paid. If the drawer discloses that he does not have the funds to cover the check, it relieves him of any guilt in the matter, and it is treated in many states as an extension of credit to the drawer. If a check is post-dated, and the drawer has asked not to have it cashed immediately, the check statutes are not violated.

EMBEZZLEMENT

At common law there was no crime of embezzlement. This too was created by statute, and was designed to cover the crime of misappropriation of property by someone to whom it had been entrusted in good faith. The various states define the crime variously, but it generally consists of fraudulent conversion, appropriation or withholding of the property of another by the one to whom it was lawfully entrusted. The embezzler usually is someone with whom there has been a relationship of trust or confidence.

In the crime of embezzlement one usually thinks of money or securities that have been unlawfully misappropriated, but personal and real property may also be taken in this manner, for example, traveler's checks executed in blank, leased personal property, or a deed to land.

The original taking must be lawful and with the consent of the owner, so the crime differs in this way from theft or larceny. Very often, however, the crime of embezzlement is included in the definition of theft, and is punished as grand or petty theft according to the value of the property taken.

The owner must have at least a recognizable legal interest, if not title, in that property. The relationship between him and the defendant must be one of trust and confidence, so the latter may be agent, employee, lessee, servant, conditional buyer, guardian, executor, bailee, as each state enumerates in its law. In the case of employees or agents, there is no difference between permanent or temporary ones.

The appropriation of the property must be done with fraudulent intent to use it in a manner the owner does not consent to. A person acting in good faith is not guilty of embezzlement, and if accused, he has a right to show that his intent is not fraudulent. Also, a person cannot embezzle his own property, so if he can show a claim of title, he is innocent.

Refusing to pay a debt is not embezzlement, nor is borrowing and keeping an object for too long a time. In the latter case if there is no direct or circumstantial evidence to show that the person has stopped being a borrower, he has not become an embezzler automatically. In some states the person must give up the article upon demand, or account for it in some way. Offering to restore embezzled money or property before being brought to court for the crime usually is considered a mitigating circumstance by the court, although in the case of larceny it does not help the defendant.

FORGERY

Forgery was a misdemeanor at common law, but it is usually a felony in our state statutes. It consists of making a false written instrument with intent to defraud, altering a genuine instrument in a material way, or uttering a forged instrument. In this sense the word "utter" means to offer or pass for value received. The "instrument" is a writing which, if genuine, would be a bill, note, or other paper which would create a legal right or obligation.

There are many ways in which the false instrument may be made. It may be printed, typed, engraved, written with pen or pencil, or it may have been genuine and then altered by erasing part, filling in a name or other words in a blank, signing another's name without authority, and the like.

There must be a writing, such as a fictitious or falsely altered check, bill, note for payment of money by a person or organization, perhaps nonexistent, and there must also be an intent to defraud. Using a genuine instrument for the purpose of defrauding another is not forgery. While it is forgery to sign another's name on a note without authority, with intent to defraud, because this makes the note seem to be the note of the person whose name as agent, falsely claiming that he has authority to bind his so-called principal. The person in that case is guilty of false pretenses, for the instrument is not a false representation, but just what it appears to be on its face. Also, to defraud another person, the instrument must appear to be true in order to defraud a person or put him at a disadvantage. If it is clearly void or illegal on its face, it is not a forgery.

While the intent to defraud is a requirement, it is not necessary that the defrauding is actually accomplished. The test is not whether anyone has been defrauded, but whether anyone might have been, unless the law of the particular state requires proof of actual injury. The intent may be inferred from circumstantial evidence, such as unauthorized signing, false explanations, or taking proceeds of the note or whatever it is for personal use.

As was stated above, "uttering" the forged instrument is passing it to another, knowing it is false. It is not necessary that the one passing it be the forger himself, if he knows of the forgery and intends to defraud by using it. The forger himself may be convicted of both forgery and uttering or of either crime, but is usually punished for only one offense where one instrument is involved. An offer as well as actual passing constitutes the crime of uttering. The maker of the false instrument himself may be guilty of uttering if he has someone else do it; he then is aiding and abetting. Several states punish the one who merely has possession of a false instrument with knowledge of its falsity and with an unlawful purpose in mind. As in other crimes, one may also be punished for attempting to utter.

COUNTERFEITING

Counterfeiting is usually thought of as unlawfully making false money in imitation of genuine coinage or paper money. The crime may also extend to other kinds of imitation, and generally covers postage stamps, notes, bank papers, tickets, certificates, counterfeiting equipment like dies and plates, and bonds.

Since issuance of coinage, stamps, etc., is the prerogative of the federal government, it is usually thought of as a federal crime, but it is also punishable under state statutes, as prosecution is not reserved to the federal courts.

Since a counterfeit is made as an imitation of the genuine article, the resemblance must be such as to deceive a person who is using ordinary caution. If there is no resemblance to a real coin, the article cannot be considered counterfeit money, for example.

Since the advent of so many vending machines requiring the use of coins, there are special statutes providing penalties for manufacturing or selling tokens or slugs which could be used to operate these machines. If a slug is used to obtain a product from a vending machine, the person doing so could be convicted of common-law larceny.

Changing color of stamps, forging overprints, using parts of cancelled stamps to produce one apparently unused stamp, are all considered counterfeiting.

Intent to defraud is not required in counterfeiting of coins, for the purpose for which the coins are made is not important. The only required intent is the intent to make the coin or stamp. But intent to defraud is required in making and passing of paper money, false obligations of securities of the government, and at times for possession of the same.

RECEIVING STOLEN PROPERTY

Receiving stolen goods, knowing them to have been stolen, was a crime at common law, and has not been changed substantially by the statutes. The crime is usually a felony, and is typically thought of as purchase of "hot" jewelry or other objects by a "fence," who conceals the goods from the police until he can sell them to another at a large profit.

The elements of the crime are that the property must have been stolen from someone, it must have been bought or received and concealed by the defendant, who must have known that it was stolen and received it for a fraudulent or unlawful purpose.

The receiver must have the property under his control, but not necessarily in his actual possession. Constructive control is all that is needed, if possession is taken by his servant or agent under his direction. The crime does not concern itself much with the thief but rather with the receiver, as the essential is that of receiving the property with the knowledge that it is stolen. The thief's identity may be unknown and is immaterial. Anyone who conceals or withholds property after learning that it is stolen is also guilty of the crime, where the statute includes the concealing of stolen property. The thief himself cannot be considered the receiver.

To convict a person of the crime it is necessary to show that the property was stolen, and that it was stolen property at the time the accused received it. He does not need to know when it was stolen or from whom. The receiver must also have a fraudulent intent in accepting the property. If he takes it with the idea of returning it to the true owner, he would not be guilty of receiving stolen property, as if he had received it for the purpose of helping the thief.

ROBBERY

Robbery, another common-law felony, is in reality a combination of larceny and assault. It may be defined as the felonious taking and carrying away of the personal property of another from his person or in his presence, against his will and by violence, or by putting him in fear. All of the elements of the crime of larceny must be present: the thing taken must be the subject of larceny and personal property belonging to another, there must be taking and carrying away, which must be with wrongful intent to deprive the owner of his property permanently. The added circumstances that make the crime robbery instead of larceny are that the property must be removed from the person of another, or in his presence or control, without his consent but also by violence or causing him to fear. Giving back the thing taken does not constitute a defense to the crime. In jurisdictions which have different degrees of the crime of robbery, first degree would involve violence or fear because of the fact that the criminal is armed with a deadly or dangerous weapon or has been torturing the victim.

If the gun looks real, but is only a toy, the offense is not mitigated by the fact that it really is a toy if it fooled the victim. If the weapon can be used as a club, it is still dangerous if not deadly. If it is not loaded, and the victim does not know this, it is dangerous, for brandishing it about in a threatening manner can cause the victim to fear. If the robber does not have a gun at first, but takes the victim's gun away from him, he is still guilty of robbery.

The requirement of taking in the presence of the victim

is usually satisfied by a taking from his constructive presence, from another room of his home, from a place where he could hear the robbers. As in the crime of larceny, the taking away need not be for a great distance or out of the presence of the victim.

There must be some slight violence at least, or putting the victim in fear. Taking the property by a trick, or by picking the victim's pocket, does not constitute violence. If the owner resists the attempt to take his property, even to a very slight degree, and his resistance is overcome, there is considered to be sufficient violence. The struggle or resistance must be during or before the taking, not after.

The requirement of fear does not mean great terror, but simply fear of injury to the victim or his family, so that he gives in to the unlawful demand for his property, under reasonable apprehension of danger. Reasonable fear of death or great bodily harm is sufficient to make the taking of property robbery. Even fear of injury to property may be sufficient, such as giving in because of a threat to burn down one's home. Fear of injury to one's character or reputation is not sufficient to make the taking of property robbery.

Chapter 4

OFFENSES AGAINST HABITATION

BURGLARY

Burglary is an offense against the security of the habitation (the man's home is his castle idea), rather than an offense against property. The purpose of this is to protect the individual in the peaceful occupancy of his home, be it cottage or mansion. At common law burglary is the breaking and entering of the dwelling house of another at night with the intent to commit a felony therein. This definition has been incorporated into criminal statutes of many states, but through the years it has been greatly modified, as a study of the charts in the appendix will show.

The word "breaking" does not necessarily mean damaging the property in any way. It is simply the opening of a door or window, one which does not even need to be locked. Coming in through an open door is not breaking, but if the defendant comes through an open front door and then opens a door that leads from a hallway to a bedroom, for example, he may be guilty of breaking and entering. If, however, he merely breaks open a box or trunk and not a part of the house, it would not be burglary. One may commit breaking and entering by coming down a chimney.

There are some instances where no breaking in the real sense as defined above takes place, but the law regards the entering as constructive entry. This may be where a person enters a house by trick or fraud, with felonious intent. Another example is where someone would pose as a policeman, or has the occupant open the door by some pretense, and he enters to commit a felony. If violence is threatened, or the owner or occupant opens the door because of fear of violence, and the defendant enters with felonious intent, there is also constructive breaking and he would be guilty of burglary. If a servant or employee in a conspiracy opens the

35

door and lets in the defendant for the purpose of committing a felony, both would be guilty of burglary.

Entry is one of the requirements for burglary as well as breaking. If no entry is made, it is not burglary to break open a door or window with intent to enter and commit a felony. This is attempted burglary. The merest entry, however, is sufficient if the felonious intent is there. It may be only a part of the body, such as a hand inserted through an open window to turn a key on a nearby door. It may even be some implement or tool, such as a hook for the purpose of stealing something.

One cannot commit burglary by breaking and entering a house or room he has a right to enter, such as a room or apartment shared with someone else, even if the person has the intent to steal his roommate's property.

At common law there was the requirement that both breaking and entering must be at nighttime, although not necessarily on the same night. In many states breaking and entering in the daytime is also punishable as burglary under the statutes, but is usually a less serious offense. Statutory changes have also added to the type of buildings where breaking and entering with felonious intent constitutes burglary. In addition to dwelling place in the strictest sense, all other sorts of habitations are included: motels, boats, mobile homes, as well as buildings like factories, schools, railroad cars, and the like.

Many courts consider that where a person enters a house without breaking and then breaks out in order to escape, it is not burglary at common law. The reason is that this is not breaking with a felonious intent, for the intent is to get away. In some of the states, however, by statute this is sufficient to constitute burglary. The laws which require breaking but not entering will cover the cases of breaking out as well as breaking in.

At common law it was not necessary for anyone to be in the house at the time of the breaking and entering, but by statute in some states the absence of a person within makes the offense less serious, such as in New York State, where there are different degrees of burglary. The house or dwelling broken into must be the house of a person other than the accused, but it may be simply another room in the same rooming house or another apartment in the building where the accused lives. A home used for only a part of a year, such as a summer cottage, may also be burglarized. The test is not ownership but lawful occupancy. The real owner of a house can commit burglary if he breaks and enters, with intent to commit a felony, a house belonging to him which he has rented to a tenant.

The intent to commit the felony may be proven by inference from the circumstances surrounding the case. If the felony was actually committed, it can be clearly inferred that the intent to commit the felony existed when the breaking and entering occurred. Even if no felony is committed, the intent may be inferred from the actions of the defendant. For example, if he breaks and enters a house at night, where there are valuable objects, and there is no other motive apparent, it may be inferred that the accused had the intent to steal, and he can be found guilty of burglary. It is not necessary that the felony be committed, for the intent is sufficient for the crime of burglary with the breaking and entering. If the felony is indeed committed, the accused may be found guilty of both the burglary and the particular felony.

In situations where not all of the elements of the crime of burglary are proven, the person may still be found guilty of other crimes, such as criminal trespass, larceny, attempted burglary, possession of burglar's tools, and attempted breaking and entering.

ARSON

Arson at common law was a felony, the malicious burning of the house of another by day or night. Punishment, appropriately enough, was death by burning at one time. Modern statutes have sometimes added the word willful, although it does not seem to mean more than malicious, nor add to the meaning, just as the words "day or night" do not actually add anything. However, under some statutes the punishment is not so severe when arson occurs in the daytime, undoubtedly because most people are awake at that time and can escape more easily.

If a person burns his own building arson is not committed in some states, but if the fire spreads and other buildings burn, he does commit unintentional arson. Here he is not acting maliciously or with ill will, but may have burned it to collect insurance. In many states burning with intent to defraud the insurer is a separate part of the arson statute, with a penalty not as serious as that for first degree arson.

Statutes in our states have also broadened the scope of the crime of arson in extending it to include buildings other than dwelling houses, such as shops, factories, unoccupied houses, one's own property, other real or personal property.

Actual burning of some part of the house or other building is required to constitute the crime. An attempt to burn by setting a fire is not enough, if the house does not burn, but the person may be punished for the attempt. No part of the building needs to be destroyed, so long as there is burning or charring of wood, even though the fire may go out by itself. Mere blackening or discoloration caused by smoke or heat is not arson.

The means used to start the fire is unimportant. It may be by setting fire to rags soaked in gasoline, simply by using matches, by using explosives if the building burns instead of merely blowing up, or by burning an adjoining structure of some kind which spreads the fire.

Where statutes have broadened the common-law definition of arson, the crime is no longer essentially a crime against security of habitation, but against property. Actual burning of some part, however, is still usually an element of the crime. Most states used the words willful or malicious or both, but usually interpret this to mean not negligently nor accidentally. Many have also divided the crime into degrees, providing the worst penalty for dwelling houses, especially when people are therein, or when the burning is at night. Attempted arson is also punishable in many jurisdictions.

Chapter 5

TYPICAL CRIMINAL PROCEDURE

When a person suspected of a crime is apprehended, what happens to him? Although the laws of the various states differ in detail, there are certain basic principles that are common to them all, and a brief outline of criminal procedure may be of interest.

THE ROLE OF THE POLICE

The police play a dual role, for they are effective not only in preventing crime, but in detecting it when committed and in seeing to it that the criminal is arrested so that he may be brought to justice. Through patrolling by car and on foot they can help prevent crime by being in areas where it is most likely to be committed, so that their presence acts as a deterrent. They respond to the complaints of citizens who are the victims of crime, and then are called upon to use scientific methods of crime detection. Where the police are well-trained, of high caliber, and are sufficient in numbers, the incidence of crime is apt to be lower than in cities where there is insufficient money to keep enough good men on the force.

Within fairly broad limits, the police have considerable discretion as to how and where they will patrol, and what kind of search they will make for criminals, and the methods of detection they will employ and what kinds of programs of crime prevention they will use.

A police officer has authority to arrest a suspect without a warrant when he has reasonable cause to believe that this suspect committed a felony, even though the officer did not see the crime being committed. In a great many states this is also the rule for misdemeanor arrests, although in some the officer must see the misdemeanor committed or have a warrant. Since 1962, when Wong Sun v. U.S., 371 U.S. 471, was decided by the United States Supreme Court, a warrant may be issued only by a judicial officer after he has weighed impartially the information which the police officer believes is probable cause for the arrest. There must be more evidence than suspicion, but not necessarily enough for conviction.[1] A mistake on the part of the police at this early stage may jeopardize the entire case if the arrest is illegal. Arresting a person known by the police to have a record of prior convictions for gambling is not probable cause.[2]

The police may use only the force believed necessary to accomplish the arrest, but an officer is acting at his own peril if he uses a gun. If the crime is a misdemeanor or there is only a suspicion of a felony, use of a gun is not justified.

The police have an implied right to stop suspected people on the street for questioning and frisking, but there is no high court decision on this matter. The circumstances must be such that there is a reasonable ground for investigation,[3] or if there is reason to believe the person to be dangerous, especially if he is searched as well as questioned. A policeman also has the right to ask a person to go with him to the police station. If the person consents, there is no unlawful detention and no arrest. Related to this is the New York "stop and frisk" law, which has also become law in other jurisdictions, and which the United States Supreme Court upheld in opinions by Chief Justice Warren.[4]

BOOKING

When the suspect is brought to a station house, the arresting policeman files a report, and the circumstances are reviewed administratively by the officer on duty or the desk ser-

---

1. See also State v. Traub, 374 U.S. 493 (1963) and Ker v. California, 374 U.S. 23 (1963).

2. Beck v. Ohio, 379 U.S. 89 (1964).

3. Compare Henry v. U.S., 361 U.S. 98 (1959) and Brinegar v. U.S., 338 U.S. 160 (1949).

4. Sibron v. New York, Peters v. New York, 392 U.S. 40 (1968); also Terry v. Ohio, 392 U.S. 1 (1968).

geant. Unless the review determines that the person should be released, he is "booked." This consists of noting on the station records a description of the suspect, the reason for his arrest, the time, the charge against him, etc. The suspect is then placed in jail. At this point he has a right to counsel.

BAIL OR DETENTION

If the suspect is accused of a misdemeanor, he may be eligible for release on bail or on "O.R." (his own recognizance), a promise to appear to answer to the charge against him at a later date. In the case of a felony, he cannot be released except after an appearance before a judicial officer. This should be done without unnecessary delay so that the person's constitutional rights under the Fifth Amendment are not violated. It is at this time that the suspect may be questioned by the police, as a part of their investigation of the crime. However, recent decisions of the United States Supreme Court have largely undermined this important means for detection of crime. Confessions obtained during overlong detention of an individual before his arraignment may be illegal;* hence they would not be admissible as evidence. In the light of recent cases it seems clear that a person may not be detained for questioning at the expense of his right to speedy arraignment, right to counsel, and right to remain silent until his lawyer or one appointed for him by the court is available.

ROLE OF THE PROSECUTOR OR DISTRICT ATTORNEY

In criminal cases the prosecuting or district attorney is the representative of the municipality or county, or in the case of appeals, of the state. He is usually elected, and serves as the chief administrator of his office, with deputy attorneys and trial attorneys working under him in felony and misdemeanor sections. In some states, such as California, the prosecutor usually plays a very important role in deciding whether or not to continue a prosecution after studying the report of the arresting officer.

---

*McNabb v. U.S., 318 U.S. 332 (1943), Mallory v. U.S., 354 U.S. 449 (1957).

He may decide, if the person is a first offender, that he should be given another chance; or if mentally ill, that he should be committed; or if the case is weak, that the prosecution should be dropped. In most major felonies, such as murder, the prosecutor's office is on the case right at the beginning, so that he can be in charge of the case and direct operations.

If the decision is to prosecute, the complaint is prepared, giving the name of the defendant and the charge, with a warrant for his arrest. In some states there must first be a meeting of the grand jury, a group of citizens whose duty it is to hear the evidence and bring an indictment to try the case, if a prima facie case has been made out, that is, if all of the evidence taken together is such as would justify a conviction if not contradicted or explained at the trial. The indictment, which is probably made out by the district attorney, is voted upon by the grand jury and filed. The defendant is not present at the convening of the grand jury.

Then the defendant's attorney is notified of the date of the arraignment to the indictment. At the arraignment the charge in the indictment is stated to the defendant and he is then asked how he pleads to it. There are several pleas that are possible: guilty, not guilty, guilty of a lesser offense, not guilty by reason of insanity, prior conviction or acquittal of that offense. The question of bail comes up again at this time, at least if the crime is a felony.

If the crime is a misdemeanor and the defendant pleads guilty, he is usually sentenced at once. If he pleads not guilty, he may be tried at once if the arresting officer and complaining witness are both present. In other cases the trial, usually without a jury, will be held in about two or three weeks.

In felony cases, the trial may not come up for several months. Then the first step will be to select the jury which should be done carefully to make sure that it is unbiased and impartial. There are rules and procedure for insuring this. The case then proceeds. First the prosecuting attorney makes an opening statement to the jury, telling the charge, the issues in the case, the evidence that will be offered to prove the case. The counsel for the defendant then makes his opening remarks, asking that the jury keep an open mind until all facts are heard. The prosecuting attorney places his witnesses on the stand first since he has the burden of proof, as it is called, to show that the defendant is guilty beyond a reasonable doubt. The witnesses are cross-examined by the opposing attorney to see if they can give any other facts that might help the defendant, or that might show whether they are lying or biased. After the prosecutor's case is presented, the defense counsel may make several motions to the court, possibly asking that the indictment be dismissed on the ground that the prosecutor has failed to prove guilt beyond a reasonable doubt. If the motions are overruled, he then presents his case for the defense, bringing out testimony and evidence favorable to the defendant, trying to explain the circumstances surrounding the case in such a way that the defendant can be excused, such as proving self-defense when there is a charge of murder against his defendant.

The prosecutor may bring a rebuttal witness, then makes his summation or closing remarks. Defense counsel will then discuss the evidence, point out inconsistencies in the prosecutor's case, comment on the testimony of witnesses and the impressions they made, and emphasize the facts which the jury should infer from the evidence to support the innocence of his client. The judge then explains the law to the jury, charging them with instructions to guide them in reaching their decision from the facts and evidence presented. When the jury's verdict is presented, the defendant is released if innocent. If found guilty, defendant has several pleas and motions available to him. His counsel may move for a new trial on the ground of error in the trial, on the ground of newly discovered evidence, etc. Another usual move is to appeal to a higher court, which reviews the record and either grants or denies the new appeal. The appeal must be made within a certain time, or it is barred. The defendant is then either set free or returned to jail to await sentencing, usually at a later date.

If the defendant had not been financially able to retain counsel, he would still have been protected under our laws, under which basically he has a constitutional right to have an attorney representing him at every stage of the proceeding in a criminal case. The court may appoint an attorney from among the members of the bar who volunteer to serve without fee. Or there may be a public defender's office or legal aid foundation, the former supported by public funds and the latter perhaps by a combination of public funds and aid from a private charitable foundation.

The defendant may also waive his right to counsel and conduct his own defense, but the court may assign counsel regardless if it considers him incompetent to act as his own attorney.

Thus every effort is made to insure that people accused of crimes are protected against injustice and given their constitutional rights.

Chapter 6

LANDMARK SUPREME COURT DECISIONS INTERPRETING THE FOURTH, FIFTH, SIXTH, AND FOURTEENTH AMENDMENTS TO THE U.S. CONSTITUTION

AMENDMENT (IV)
The right of the people to be secure in their persons, houses, papers, and effects, against unreasonable searches and seizures, shall not be violated, and no Warrants shall issue, but upon probable cause, supported by Oath or affirmation, and particularly describing the place to be searched, and the persons or things to be seized.

> Mapp v. Ohio
> Sibron v. N.Y. and Peters v. N.Y.
> Terry v. Ohio
> Chimel v. California

AMENDMENT (V)
No person shall be held to answer for a capital, or otherwise infamous crime, unless on a presentment or indictment of a Grand Jury, except in cases arising in the land or naval forces, or in the Militia, when in actual service in time of War or public danger; nor shall any person be subject for the same offense to be twice put in jeopardy of life or limb; nor shall be compelled in any criminal case to be a witness against himself, nor be deprived of life, liberty, or property, without due process of law; nor shall private property be taken for public use, without just compensation.

> Mapp v. Ohio
> Miranda v. Arizona

AMENDMENT (VI)

In all criminal prosecutions, the accused shall enjoy the right to a speedy and public trial, by an impartial jury of the State and district wherein the crime shall have been committed, which district shall have been previously ascertained by law, and to be informed of the nature and cause of the accusation; to be confronted with the witnesses against him; to have compulsory process for obtaining Witnesses in his favor, and to have the Assistance of Counsel for his defence.

> Escobedo v. Illinois
> Gideon v. Wainwright (see Escobedo)

AMENDMENT (XIV)

Section 1. All persons born or naturalized in the United States and subject to the jurisdiction thereof, are citizens of the United States and of the State wherein they reside. No State shall make or enforce any law which shall abridge the privileges or immunities of citizens of the United States; nor shall any State deprive any person of life, liberty, or property, without due process of law; nor deny to any person within its jurisdiction the equal protection of the laws.

> Sibron v. N.Y. and Peters v. N.Y.

MAPP v. OHIO
367 U.S. 643 (1961)

Appellant stands convicted of knowingly having had in her possession and under her control certain lewd and lascivious books, pictures, and photographs in violation of § 2905.34 of Ohio's Revised Code. As officially stated in the syllabus to its opinion, the Supreme Court of Ohio found that her conviction was valid though "based primarily upon the introduction in evidence of lewd and lascivious books and pictures unlawfully seized during an unlawful search of defendant's home . . . ." 170 Ohio St. 427-428, 166 N.E. 2d 387, 388.

. . . .

. . . . When Miss Mapp did not come to the door immediately, at least one of the several doors to the house was forcibly opened and the policemen gained admittance. Meanwhile Miss

Mapp's attorney arrived, but the officers, having secured their own entry, and continuing in their defiance of the law, would permit him neither to see Miss Mapp nor to enter the house . . . . A paper, claimed to be a warrant, was held up by one of the officers. She grabbed the "warrant" and placed it in her bosom. A struggle ensued in which the officers recovered the piece of paper and as a result of which they handcuffed appellant because she had been "belligerent" in resisting their official rescue of the "warrant" from her person . . . . Appellant, in handcuffs, was then forcibly taken upstairs to her bedroom where the officers searched a dresser, a chest of drawers, a closet and some suitcases . . . . The search spread to the rest of the second floor . . . . The basement of the building and a trunk found therein were also searched. The obscene materials for possession of which she was ultimately convicted were discovered in the course of that widespread search.

At the trial no search warrant was produced by the prosecution, nor was the failure to produce one explained or accounted for . . . .

The State says that even if the search were made without authority, or otherwise unreasonably, it is not prevented from using the unconstitutionally seized evidence at trial, citing Wolf v. Colorado, 338 U.S. 25 (1949), in which this Court did indeed hold "that in a prosecution in a State court for a State crime the Fourteenth Amendment does not forbid the admission of evidence obtained by an unreasonable search and seizure."

Seventy-five years ago, in Boyd v. United States, 116 U.S. 616, 630 (1886), considering the Fourth and Fifth Amendments as running "almost into each other" on the facts before it, this Court held that the doctrines of those Amendments

"apply to all invasions on the part of the government and its employees of the sanctity of a man's home and the privacies of life . . . . Breaking into a house and opening boxes and drawers are circumstances of aggravation; but any forcible and compulsory extortion of a man's own testimony or of his private papers to be used as evidence to convict him of crime or to forfeit his goods, is within the condemnation . . . (of those Amendments)."

. . . .

Since the Fourth Amendment's right of privacy has been declared enforceable against the States through the Due Process Clause of the Fourteenth, it is enforceable against them by the same sanction of exclusion as is used against the Federal Government. At the time that the Court held in Wolf that the Amendment was applicable to the States through the Due Process Clause, the cases of this Court, as we have seen, had steadfastly held that as to federal officers the Fourth Amendment included the exclusion of the evidence seized in violation of its provisions.

. . . .

. . . The admission of the new constitutional right by Wolf could not consistently tolerate denial of its most important constitutional privilege, namely, the exclusion of the evidence which an accused had been forced to give by reason of the unlawful seizure. To hold otherwise is to grant the right but in reality to withhold the privilege and enjoyment. Only last year the Court itself recognized that the purpose of the exclusionary rule "is to deter--to compel respect for the constitutional guaranty in the only effectively available way--by removing the incentive to disregard it." Elkins v. United States, supra, at p. 217.

. . . And nothing could be more certain than that when a coerced confession is involved, "the relevant rules of evidence" are overridden without regard to "the incidence of such conduct by the police," slight or frequent. Why should not the same rule apply to what is tantamount to coerced testimony by way of unconstitutional seizure of goods, papers, effects, documents, etc.? We find that, as to the Federal Government, the Fourth and Fifth Amendments and, as to the States, the freedom from unconscionable invasions of privacy and the freedom from convictions based upon coerced confessions do enjoy an "intimate relation" in their perpetuation of "principles of humanity and civil liberty (secured) . . . only after years of struggle," Bram v. United States, 168 U.S. 532, 543-544 (1897) . . . . The philosophy of each Amendment and of each freedom is complementary to, although not dependent upon, that of the other in its sphere of influence--the very least that together they assure in either sphere is that no man is to be convicted on unconstitutional evidence . . . .

Moreover, our holding that the exclusionary rule is an essential part of both the Fourth and Fourteenth Amendments is not only the logical dictate of prior cases, but it also makes very good sense. There is no war between the Constitution and common sense. Presently, a federal prosecutor may make no use of evidence illegally seized, but a State's attorney across the street may, although he supposedly is operating under the enforceable prohibitions of the same Amendment. Thus the State, by admitting evidence unlawfully seized, serves to encourage disobedience to the Federal Constitution which it is bound to uphold.

. . . .

ESCOBEDO v. ILLINOIS
378 U.S. 478 (1964)

The critical question in this case is whether, under the circumstances, the refusal by the police to honor petitioner's request to consult with his lawyer during the course of an interrogation constitutes a denial of "the Assistance of Counsel" in violation of the Sixth Amendment to the Constitution as "made obligatory upon the States by the Fourteenth Amendment," Gideon v. Wainwright, 372 U.S. 335, 342, and thereby renders inadmissible in a state criminal trial any incriminating statement elicited by the police during the interrogation.

. . . .

The interrogation here was conducted before petitioner was formally indicted. But in the context of this case, that fact should make no difference. When petitioner requested, and was denied, an opportunity to consult with his lawyer, the investigation had ceased to be a general investigation of "an unsolved crime." Spano v. New York, 360 U.S. 315, 327 (Stewart, J., concurring). Petitioner had become the accused, and the purpose of the interrogation was to "get him" to confess his guilt despite his constitutional right not to do so. At the time of his arrest and throughout the course of the interrogation, the police told petitioner that they had convincing evidence that he had fired the fatal shots. Without informing him of his absolute right to remain silent in the face of this accusation, the police urged him to make a statement . . . . Petitioner, a layman, was undoubtedly unaware that under Illinois law an admission of "mere" complicity in the murder plot was legally as damaging as an admission of firing the fatal

49

shots. Illinois v. Escobedo, 28 Ill. 2d 41, 190 N.E. 2d 825....
This was the "stage when legal aid and advice" were most critical
to petitioner . . . .

In Gideon v. Wainwright, 372 U.S. 335, we held that every
person accused of a crime, whether state or federal, is entitled
to a lawyer at trial. The rule sought by the State here, however,
would make the trial no more than an appeal from the interrogation; and the "right to use counsel at the formal trial (would be)
a very hollow thing (if), for all practical purposes, the conviction
is already assured by pretrial examination." In re Groban, 352
U.S. 330, 344 . . . .

It is argued that if the right to counsel is afforded prior to
indictment, the number of confessions obtained by the police will
diminish significantly, because most confessions are obtained
during the period between arrest and indictment . . . . The right
to counsel would indeed be hollow if it began at a period when few
confessions were obtained. There is necessarily a direct relationship between the importance of a stage to the police in their quest
for a confession and the criticalness of that stage to the accused
in his need for legal advice. Our Constitution, unlike some others,
strikes the balance in favor of the right of the accused to be advised by his lawyer of his privilege against self-incrimination....

We have learned the lesson of history, ancient and modern,
that a system of criminal law enforcement which comes to depend
on the "confession" will, in the long run, be less reliable and more
subject to abuses than a system which depends on extrinsic evidence independently secured through skillful investigation . . . .

We have also learned the companion lesson of history that
no system of criminal justice can, or should, survive if it comes
to depend for its continued effectiveness on the citizen's abdication
through unawareness of their constitutional rights . . . .

We hold, therefore, that where, as here, the investigation
is no longer a general inquiry into an unsolved crime but has begun
to focus on a particular suspect, the suspect has been taken into
police custody, the police carry out a process of interrogations
that lends itself to eliciting incriminating statements, the suspect
has requested and been denied an opportunity to consult with his
lawyer, and the police have not effectively warned him of his absolute constitutional right to remain silent, the accused has been
denied "the Assistance of Counsel" in violation of the Sixth Amend-

ment to the Constitution as "made obligatory upon the States by the Fourteenth Amendment, " Gideon v. Wainwright, 372 U.S., at 342, and that no statement elicited by the police during the interrogation may be used against him at a criminal trial.

. . . .

Nothing we have said today affects the powers of the police to investigate "an unsolved crime, " Spano v. New York, 360 U.S. 315, 327 (Stewart, J., concurring), by gathering information from witnesses and by other "proper investigative efforts." Haynes v. Washington, 373 U.S. 503, 519. We hold only that when the process shifts from investigatory to accusatory--when its focus is on the accused and its purpose is to elicit a confession--our adversary system begins to operate, and, under the circumstances here, the accused must be permitted to consult with his lawyer.

. . . .

MIRANDA v. ARIZONA
384 U.S. 436 (1966)

. . . We deal with the admissibility of statements obtained from an individual who is subjected to custodial police interrogation and the necessity for procedures which assure that the individual is accorded his privilege under the Fifth Amendment to the Constitution not to be compelled to incriminate himself.

We dealt with certain phases of this problem recently in Escobedo v. Illinois, 378 U.S. 478 (1964). There, as in the four cases before us, law enforcement officials took the defendant into custody and interrogated him in a police station for the purpose of obtaining a confession. The police did not effectively advise him of his right to remain silent or of his right to consult with his attorney.

. . . .

This case has been the subject of judicial interpretation and spirited legal debate since it was decided two years ago . . . . We granted certiorari in these cases, 382 U.S. 924, 925, 937, in order further to explore some facets of the problems thus exposed . . . .

. . . .

The constitutional issue we decide in each of these cases is the admissibility of statements obtained from a defendant questioned while in custody or otherwise deprived of his freedom of action in any significant way. In each, the defendant was questioned by police officers, detectives, or a prosecuting attorney in a room in which he was cut off from the outside world. In none of these cases was the defendant given a full and effective warning of his rights at the outset of the interrogation process. In all the cases, the questioning elicited oral admissions, and in three of them, signed statements as well which were admitted at their trials. They all thus share salient features--incommunicado interrogation of individuals in a police-dominated atmosphere, resulting in self-incriminating statements without full warnings of constitutional rights.

. . . .

In these cases, we might not find the defendant's statements to have been involuntary in traditional terms. Our concern for adequate safeguards to protect precious Fifth Amendment rights is, of course, not lessened in the slightest. In each of the cases, the defendant was thrust into an unfamiliar atmosphere and run through menacing police interrogation procedures. The potentiality for compulsion is forcefully apparent . . . . To be sure, the records do not evince overt physical coercion or patent psychological ploys. The fact remains that in none of these cases did the officers undertake to afford appropriate safeguards at the outset to afford appropriate safeguards at the outset of the interrogation to insure that the statements were truly the product of free choice.

It is obvious that such an interrogation environment is created for no purpose other than to subjugate the individual to the will of his examiner. This atmosphere carries its own badge of intimidation. To be sure, this is not physical intimidation, but it is equally destructive of human dignity . . . .

. . . The denial of the defendant's request for his attorney thus undermined his ability to exercise the privilege--to remain silent if he chose or to speak without any intimidation, blatant or subtle. The presence of counsel, in all the cases before us today, would be the adequate protective device necessary to make the process of police interrogation conform to the dictates of the privilege . . . .

. . . .

. . . We have concluded that without proper safeguards the process of in-custody interrogation of persons suspected or accused
of crime contains inherently compelling pressures which work to
undermine the individual's will to resist and to compel him to
speak where he would not otherwise do so freely. In order to
combat these pressures and to permit a full opportunity to exercise the privilege against self-incrimination, the accused must
be adequately and effectively apprised of his rights and the exercise of those rights must be fully honored.

. . . .

Unless we are shown other procedures which are at least as
effective in apprising accused persons of their right of silence
and in assuring a continuous opportunity to exercise it, the following safeguards must be observed.

At the outset, if a person in custody is to be subjected to
interrogation, he must first be informed in clear and unequivocal
terms that he has the right to remain silent. For those unaware
of the privilege, the warning is needed simply to make them aware
of it--the threshold requirement for an intelligent decision as to
its exercise. More important, such a warning is an absolute pre-
requisite in overcoming the inherent pressures of the interrogation atmosphere . . . .

. . . .

The warning of the right to remain silent must be accompanied by the explanation that anything said can and will be used
against the individual in court. This warning is needed in order
to make him aware not only of the privilege, but also of the consequences of foregoing it. It is only through an awareness of these
consequences that there can be any assurance of real understanding and intelligent exercise of the privilege. Moreover, this
warning may serve to make the individual more acutely aware
that he is faced with a phase of the adversary system--that he is
not in the presence of persons acting solely in his interest.

The circumstances surrounding in-custody interrogation
can operate very quickly to overbear the will of one merely made
aware of his privilege by his interrogators. Therefore, the right
to have counsel present at the interrogation is indispensable to

53

the protection of the Fifth Amendment privilege under the system we delineate today. Our aim is to assure that the individual's right to choose between silence and speech remains unfettered throughout the interrogation process . . . .

If an individual indicates that he wishes the assistance of counsel before any interrogation occurs, the authorities cannot rationally ignore or deny his request on the basis that the individual does not have or cannot afford a retained attorney . . . . Denial of counsel to the indigent at the time of interrogation while allowing an attorney to those who can afford one would be no more supportable by reason or logic than the similar situation at trial and on appeal struck down in Gideon v. Wainwright, 372 U.S. 335 (1963), and Douglas v. California, 372 U.S. 353 (1963).

In order fully to apprise a person interrogated of the extent of his rights under this system then, it is necessary to warn him not only that he has the right to consult with an attorney, but also that if he is indigent a lawyer will be appointed to represent him. Without this additional warning, the admonition of the right to consult with counsel would often be understood as meaning only that he can consult with a lawyer if he has one or has the funds to obtain one . . . .

. . . .

SIBRON v. NEW YORK, PETERS v. NEW YORK
392 U.S. 40 (1968)

. . . It is difficult to conceive of stronger grounds for an arrest, short of actual eyewitness observations of criminal activity. As the trial court explicitly recognized, deliberately furtive actions and flight at the approach of strangers or law officers are strong indicia of mens rea, and when coupled with specific knowledge on the part of the officer relating the suspect to the evidence of crime, they are proper factors to be considered in the decision to make an arrest . . . .

As we noted in Sibron's case, a search incident to a lawful arrest may not precede the arrest and serve as part of its justification . . . . . it is clear that the arrest had, for purposes of constitutional justification, already taken place before the search commenced. When the policeman grabbed Peters by the collar, he abruptly "seized" him and curtailed his freedom of movement

54

on the basis of probable cause to believe that he was engaged in criminal activity. At that point he had the authority to search Peters, and the incident search was obviously justified "by the need to seize weapons and other things which might be used to assault an officer or effect an escape, as well as by the need to prevent the destruction of evidence of the crime." Preston v. United States, 376 U.S. 364, 367 (1964). Moreover, it was reasonably limited in scope by these purposes. Officer Lasky did not engage in an unrestrained and thoroughgoing examination of Peters and his personal effects. He seized him to cut short his flight, and he searched him primarily for weapons. While patting down his outer clothing, Officer Lasky discovered an object in his pocket which might have been used as a weapon. He seized it and discovered it to be a potential instrument of the crime of burglary.

We have concluded that Peters' conviction fully comports with the commands of the Fourth and Fourteenth Amendments and must be affirmed.

. . . .

TERRY v. OHIO
392 U.S. 1 (1968)

. . . . . The State has characterized the issue here as "the right of a police officer . . . to make an on-the-street stop, interrogate and pat down for weapons (known in street vernacular as 'stop and frisk')." But this is only partly accurate. For the issue is not the abstract propriety of the police conduct, but the admissibility against petitioner of the evidence uncovered by the search and seizure. Ever since its inception, the rule excluding evidence seized in violation of the Fourth Amendment has been recognized as a principal mode of discouraging lawless police conduct . . . . . experience has taught that it is the only effective deterrent to police misconduct in the criminal context, and that without it the constitutional guarantee against unreasonable searches and seizures would be a mere "form of words." Mapp v. Ohio, 367 U.S. 643, 655 (1961). The rule also serves another vital function--"the imperative of judicial integrity." Elkins v. United States, 364 U.S. 206, 222 (1960). Courts which sit under our Constitution cannot and will not be made party to lawless invasions of the constitutional rights of citizens by permitting unhindered governmental use of the fruits of such invasions. Thus in our system evidentiary rulings provide the context in which the judicial process of inclusion and exclusion approves some conduct as comporting with constitutional guarantees and disapproves other actions by state agents . . . . Street encounters between citizens and police officers are incredibly rich in diversity . . . . Encounters are initiated by the police for a wide variety of purposes, some of which are wholly unrelated to a desire to prosecute for crime. . . .

Our first task is to establish at what point in this encounter the Fourth Amendment becomes relevant. That is, we must decide whether and when Officer McFadden "seized" Terry and whether and when he conducted a "search." There is some suggestion in the use of such terms as "stop" and "frisk" that such police conduct is outside the purview of the Fourth Amendment because neither action rises to the level of a "search" or "seizure" within the meaning of the Constitution. We emphatically reject this notion. It is quite plain that the Fourth Amendment governs "seizures" of the person which do not eventuate in a trip to the station house and prosecution for crime--"arrests" in traditional terminology. It must be recognized that whenever a police officer accosts an individual and restrains his freedom to walk away, he has "seized" that person. And it is nothing less than sheer torture of the English language to suggest that a careful exploration of the outer surfaces of a person's clothing all over his or her body in an attempt to find weapons is not a "search" . . . . . it is not to be undertaken lightly.

The danger in the logic which proceeds upon distinctions between a "stop" and an "arrest," or "seizure" of the person, and between a "frisk" and a "search" is twofold. It seeks to isolate from constitutional scrutiny the initial stages of the contact between the policeman and the citizen. And by suggestion a rigid all-or-nothing model of justification and regulation under the Amendment, it obscures the utility of limitations upon the scope, as well as the initiation, of police action as a means of constitutional regulation . . . . (The search) must be limited to that which is necessary for the discovery of weapons which might be used to harm the officer or others nearby, and may realistically be characterized as something less than a "full" search, even though it remains a serious intrusion. . . . An arrest is a wholly different kind of intrusion upon individual freedom from a limited search for weapons, and the interests each is designed to serve are likewise quite different. An arrest is the initial stage of a criminal prosecution. It is intended to vindicate society's interest in having its laws obeyed, and it is inevitably accompanied by future interference with the individual's freedom of movement, whether or not trial or conviction ultimately follows. The protective search for weapons, on the other hand, constitutes a brief, though far from inconsiderable, intrusion upon the sanctity of the person. It does not follow that because an officer may lawfully arrest a person only when he is apprised of facts sufficient to warrant a belief that the person has committed or is committing a crime, the officer is equally unjustified, absent that kind of evidence, in making any intrusions short of an arrest. Moreover, a perfectly reasonable apprehension of danger may arise long before the officer is possessed of adequate information to justify taking a person into custody for the purpose of prosecuting him for a crime.

. . . .

Our evaluation of the proper balance that has to be struck in this type of case leads us to conclude that there must be a narrowly drawn authority to permit a reasonable search for weapons for the protection of the police officer, where he has reason to believe that he is dealing with an armed and dangerous individual, regardless of whether he has probable cause to arrest the individual for a crime. The officer need not be absolutely certain that the individual is armed; the issue is whether a reasonably prudent man in the circumstances would be warranted in the belief that his safety or that of others was in danger. Cf. Beck v. Ohio, 379 U.S. 89, 91 (1964); Brinegar v. United States, 338 U.S. 160, 174-176 (1949); Stacey v. Emery, 97 U.S. 642, 645 (1878). And in determining whether the officer acted reasonably in such circumstances, due weight must be given, not to his inchoate and unparticularized suspicion or "hunch," but to the specific reasonable inferences which he is entitled to draw from the facts in light of his experience. Cf. Brinegar v. United States supra.

. . . .

We conclude that the revolver seized from Terry was properly admitted in evidence against him . . . . Each case of this sort will, of course, have to be decided on its own facts. We merely hold today that where a police officer observes unusual conduct which leads him reasonably to conclude in light of his experience that criminal activity may be afoot and that the persons with whom he is dealing may be armed and presently dangerous, where in the course of investigating this behavior he identifies himself as a policeman and makes reasonable inquiries, and where nothing in the initial stages of the encounter serves to dispel his reasonable fear for his own or others' safety, he is entitled for the protection of himself and others in the area to conduct a carefully limited search of the outer clothing of such persons in an attempt to discover weapons which might be used to assault him. Such a search is a reasonable search under the Fourth Amendment, and any weapons seized may properly be introduced in evidence against the person from whom they were taken.

· · · · · · ·

CHIMEL v. CALIFORNIA
395 U.S. 752 (1969)

. . . When an arrest is made, it is reasonable for the arresting officer to search the person arrested in order to remove any weapons that the latter might seek to use in order to resist arrest or effect his escape. Otherwise, the officer's safety might well be endangered, and the arrest itself frustrated. In addition, it is entirely reasonable for the arresting officer to search for and seize any evidence on the arrestee's person in order to prevent its concealment or destruction. And the area into which an arrestee might reach in order to grab a weapon or evidentiary items must, of course, be governed by a like rule. A gun on a table or in a drawer in front of one who is arrested can be as dangerous to the arresting officer as one concealed in the clothing of the person arrested. There is ample justification, therefore, for a search of the arrestee's person and the area "within his immediate control" --construing that phrase to mean the area from within which he might gain possession of a weapon or destructible evidence.

There is no comparable justification, however, for routinely searching any room other than that in which an arrest occurs-- or, for that matter, for searching through all the desk drawers or other closed or concealed areas in that room itself. Such searches, in the absence of well-recognized exceptions, may be made only under the authority of a search warrant. The "adherence to judicial processes" mandated by the Fourth Amendment requires no less.

· · · · · · ·

It is argued in the present case that it is "reasonable" to search a man's house when he is arrested in it. But that argument is founded on little more than a subjective view regarding the acceptability of certain sorts of police conduct, and not on considerations relevant to Fourth Amendment interests. Under such an unconfined analysis, Fourth Amendment protection in this area would approach the evaporation point. It is not easy to explain why, for instance, it is less subjectively "reasonable" to search a man's house when he is arrested on his front lawn--or just down the street--than it is when he happens to be in the house at the time of arrest. . . . No consideration relevant to the Fourth Amendment suggests any point of rational limitation, once the search is allowed to go beyond the area from which the person arrested might obtain weapons or evidentiary items. The only reasoned distinction is one between a search of the person arrested and the area within his reach on the one hand, and more extensive searches on the other.

· · · · · · ·

Application of sound Fourth Amendment principles to the facts of this case produces a clear result. The search here went far beyond the petitioner's person and the area from within which he might have obtained either a weapon or something that could have been used as evidence against him. There was no constitutional justification, in the absence of a search warrant, for extending the search beyond that area. The scope of the search was, therefore, "unreasonable" under the Fourth and Fourteenth Amendments, and the petitioner's conviction cannot stand.

Table No. 1

MURDER AND MANSLAUGHTER
DEFINITIONS AND PENALTIES

ALABAMA
Murder--First Deg.: Perpetrated by poison, lying in waiting or any other kind of willful, deliberate, malicious and premeditated killing; or committed in perpetration or attempt to perpetrate any arson, rape, robbery or burglary; or from a premeditated design unlawfully and maliciously to effect the death of any human other than one killed; or by act greatly dangerous to lives of others and evidencing a depraved mind regardless of human life.

Death or life imprisonment.

Second Deg.: Every other homicide, as would be murder at common law.

Not less than 10 years.

Manslaughter--First Deg.: Voluntary depriving a human of life.

Second Deg.: Manslaughter under any other circumstance.

Up to 1 year and up to $500.

Code of Alabama, Tit. 14, §§ 314-323

ALASKA
Murder--First Deg.: Killing another out of deliberate and premeditated malice, or by means of poison, or in perpetrating or attempting to perpetrate rape, arson, robbery, or burglary.

Imprisonment at hard labor for life or for any term of years.

ALASKA (continued)

Second Deg.: Killing another purposely and maliciously.
Not less than 15 years.

Manslaughter: Unlawfully killing another.
1 to 20 years.

Alaska Statutes, 11.15.010-11.15.040

ARIZONA

Murder: First Deg.: Perpetrated by poison, lying in wait, torture or other kind of willful, deliberate and premeditated killing, committed in perpetration or attempt to perpetrate of arson, rape, robbery, burglary or mayhem.
Death or life imprisonment.

Second Deg.: All other kinds of murder.
Not less than 10 years.

Manslaughter: Unlawful killing of human being without malice.

Voluntary: Upon sudden quarrel or heat of passion.

Involuntary: In commission of unlawful act not a felony or in lawful act which might produce death in an unlawful manner, or without due caution.
Up to 10 years.

Arizona Rev. Code, §§ 43-2901 to 2903

ARKANSAS

Murder: Unlawful killing of a human being, with malice aforethough, either express or implied.

First Deg.: Perpetrated by means of poison, or by lying in wait, or by any other willful, deliberate, malicious and premeditated killing, or committed in the perpetration or attempt to perpetrate arson, rape, robbery, burglary or larceny.
Death (by hanging) or life imprisonment.

Second Deg.: All other murder.
5 to 21 years.

Manslaughter: Unlawful killing, without malice express or implied, and without deliberation.

Voluntary: Upon sudden heat of passion, caused by a provocation, apparently sufficient to make passion irresistible.
2 to 7 years.

61

Involuntary: In commission of unlawful act, without malice, and without means calculated to produce death, or in prosecution of lawful act, done without due caution and circumspection.

> Up to 3 years and/or $100 to $1000.
> Arkansas Statutes, 1947, Chapter 22,
> §§ 41-2201 to 2209
> 41-2227 to 2230

CALIFORNIA

Murder: Unlawful killing of a human being, with malice aforethought.

First Deg.: Perpetrated by means of poison, or lying in wait, torture, or by any other kind of willful, deliberate, and premeditated killing, or which is committed in the perpetration or attempt to perpetrate arson, rape, robbery, burglary or mayhem.

> Death or life imprisonment.

Second Deg.: All other kinds of murder.

> 5 years to life.

Manslaughter: Unlawful killing of a human being without malice.

1. Voluntary--upon a sudden quarrel or heat of passion.

2. Involuntary--in the commission of an unlawful act, not amounting to felony; or in the commission of a lawful act which might produce death, in an unlawful manner, or without due caution and circumspection; provided that this subdivision shall not apply to acts committed in the driving of a vehicle.

3. In the driving of a vehicle--

(a) In the commission of an unlawful act, not amounting to felony, with gross negligence; or in the commission of a lawful act which might produce death, in an unlawful manner, and with gross negligence.

(b) In the commission of an unlawful act, not amounting to felony, without gross negligence; or in the commission of a lawful act which might produce death, in an unlawful manner, but without gross negligence.

> Up to 15 years for voluntary or involuntary manslaughter.

CALIFORNIA (continued)

For negligent homicide in 3, 1-5 years for a, up to 1 year for b.

California Penal Code, §§ 187-192

COLORADO

Murder: Unlawful killing of a human being with malice aforethought, either express or implied.

First Deg.: Perpetrated by means of poison or lying in wait, torture, or by any kind of willful, deliberate and premeditated killing; or committed in perpetration or attempt to perpetrate arson, rape, robbery, mayhem or burglary; or from a deliberate and premeditated design, unlawfully and maliciously, to effect the death of any human being other than one killed; or by act greatly dangerous to the lives of others and indicating a depraved mind, regardless of human life.

Life imprisonment.

Second Deg.: All other kinds of murder.

10 years to life.

Manslaughter: Unlawful killing without malice or deliberation; voluntary, sudden heat or irresistible passion or due to injury inflicted upon the one killing; involuntary, in committing act without due caution.

Voluntary: 1-8 years.

Involuntary: Up to 1 year.

Colorado Rev. Statutes, 1963,
40-2-3 to 40-2-8

CONNECTICUT

Murder--First Deg.: All murder perpetrated by means of poison, or by lying in wait, or by any other kind of willful, deliberate and premeditated killing, or committed in perpetrating or in attempting to perpetrate any arson, rape, robbery or burglary or injury to any person or property by means of any explosive compound.

Death or life imprisonment.

Second Deg.: All other kinds of murder.

Life imprisonment.

CONNECTICUT (continued)

Manslaughter: Not defined.

Up to $1000 and/or up to 15 years.

General Statutes of Connecticut, 1958,
53-9 to 53-13

DELAWARE

Murder--First Deg: Murder with express malice aforethought or in perpetrating, or attempting to perpetrate, rape, kidnaping, treason, etc.

Death.

Second Deg.: Other murders.

Life imprisonment.

Manslaughter: Not defined (except that manslaughter by
husband of person found in act of adultery with wife is misdemeanor, penalty being fine of $100 to $1,000 and imprisonment
up to one year).

Up to 30 years, or up to $10,000.

Delaware Code Annotated, §§ 11-571 to
11-575

FLORIDA

Murder--First Deg.: When perpetrated from a premeditated design to effect the death of the person killed or any human
being, or when committed in the perpetration or attempt to perpetrate any arson, rape, robbery, or burglary.

Death.

Second Deg.: By act imminently dangerous to another,
evincing a depraved mind regardless of human life, although without any premeditated design to effect the death of any particular
individual.

Life or not less than 20 years.

Third Deg.: Without any design to effect death, by a person engaged in the commission of any felony, other than arson,
rape, robbery, or burglary.

Up to 20 years.

Manslaughter: By act, procurement or culpable negligence
of another, in cases where such killings are not justifiable or

FLORIDA (continued)
excusable homicide nor murder.
>Up to 20 years or up to $5,000.
>>Florida Statutes Annotated, 1941,
>>>Title 44, § 782.04

GEORGIA
>Murder: Unlawful killing of a human being by a person of sound memory and discretion, with malice aforeghought, either express or implied.
>>Death or life imprisonment.
>Manslaughter: Without malice, either express or implied, and without any mixture of deliberation whatever, which may be voluntary, upon a sudden heat of passion, or involuntary, in the commission of an unlawful act, or a lawful act without due caution and circumspection.
>>Voluntary
>>>1 to 20 years.
>>Involuntary, in commission of unlawful act.
>>>1 to 5 years.
>>Involuntary, lawful act.
>>>As for misdemeanor.
>>>Georgia Statutes Annotated,
>>>>§§ 26-1102 to 1104

HAWAII
>Murder: First Deg.: Killing without authority, justification or extenuation of law, with deliberate premeditated malice aforethought, with malice aforethought and with extreme cruelty or atrocity, or in connection with crimes or attempt to crime of arson, rape, robbery, burglary or kidnaping.
>>Life imprisonment at hard labor without parole.
>>Second Deg.: Killing with malice aforethought.
>>>Hard labor for not less than 20 years.
>>Manslaughter: Killing without malice aforethought.
>>>Hard labor for not more than 10 years.
>>>>Hawaii Rev. Statutes, 748-1 to 748-7

IDAHO

Murder--First Deg.: Perpetrated by means of poison, or lying in wait, torture, or by any other kind of willful, deliberate and premeditated killing, or which is committed in the perpetration of, or attempt to perpetrate, arson, rape, robbery, burglary, kidnaping or mayhem.

Death or life imprisonment.

Second Deg.: All other kinds of murder.

10 years to life.

Manslaughter: Unlawful killing without malice.

Voluntary: Upon sudden quarrel or heat of passion.

Up to 10 years, or $2,000 or both.

Involuntary: In perpetration or attempt to perpetrate unlawful act, other than arson, rape, robbery, kidnaping, burblary, or mayhem; or in commission of unlawful act which might produce death, in an unlawful manner, or without due caution and circumspection; operation of motor vehicle in reckless, careless manner, or operation of any deadly weapon in reckless, careless manner.

Up to $1,000 and/or up to 10 years.

Idaho Code, 1947, §§ 18-4003, 4004, 4006, 4007

ILLINOIS

Murder: Killing without lawful justification if in performing the acts which cause death, the killer intends to kill or do great bodily harm to that person or knows such acts will cause death, or strong probability of death, or killing while committing forcible entry, other than manslaughter.

Death or imprisonment not less than 14 years.

Voluntary Manslaughter: Killing without lawful justification under sudden or intense passion resulting from serious provocation by the individual he attempts to kill, negligently or accidentally causing death to another; intentionally or knowingly kills one believing circumstances if they existed would exonerate him, but such belief is unreasonable.

1 to 20 years.

Involuntary Manslaughter: Killing without lawful justification if acts lawful or unlawful are such as are likely to cause

ILLINOIS (continued)
death or great bodily harm, and he performs them recklessly.
>1 to 10 years.
>>Illinois Statutes Anno., 38 §§ 9-1 to 9-3

INDIANA
>Murder--First Deg.: Purposely and with premeditated malice or in the perpetration of or attempt to perpetrate a rape, arson, robbery or burglary.
>>Death or life imprisonment.
>Second Deg.: Purposely and maliciously, but without premeditation.
>>Life imprisonment.
>Manslaughter: Voluntarily kills without malice, expressed or implied, in a sudden heat or involuntarily in the commission of some unlawful act.
>>2 to 21 years.
>>>Burns Indiana Statutes, 1933, §§ 10-3401, 3404, 3405

IOWA
>Murder: Malice aforethought, either express or implied.
>First Deg.: Perpetrated by means of poison, or lying in wait, or any other kind of willful, deliberate and premeditated killing, or which is committed in the perpetration or attempt to perpetrate any arson, rape, robbery, mayhem or burglary.
>>Life imprisonment.
>Second Deg.: Other murder.
>>Life or not less than 10 years.
>Manslaughter: No definition.
>>Up to 8 years and up to $1,000 fine.
>>>Iowa Code, Anno. §§ 690.1, 690.2, 690.3, 690.10

KANSAS
>Murder--First Deg.: Committed by means of poison or by lying in wait, or by any kind of willful, deliberate and premeditated killing, or which shall be committed in the perpetration or

KANSAS (continued)
an attempt to perpetrate any arson, rape, robbery, burglary, or other felony.

Death or life imprisonment.

Second Deg.: Committed purposely and maliciously but without deliberation and premeditation.

Not less than 10 years.

Kansas Statutes Anno., 1949, §§ 21-401, 402, 403

KENTUCKY

Murder: No definition except "willful murder."

Death or life imprisonment.

Voluntary Manslaughter: No definition.

2 to 21 years.

Baldwin's Kentucky Revised Statutes Ann.
§§ 435.010, 435.020

LOUISIANA

Murder: When the offender has a specific intent to kill or to inflict great bodily harm; or when the offender is engaged in the perpetration or attempted perpetration of aggravated arson, aggravated burglary, aggravated kidnaping, aggravated rape, armed robbery, or simple robbery, even though he has no intent to kill.

Death.

Manslaughter: Committed in sudden passion or heat of blood immediately caused by provocation sufficient to deprive an average person of his self-control and cool reflection; homicide committed without any intent to cause death or great bodily harm when the offender is engaged in perpetration or attempted perpetration of any felony (not included in the list under murder) or any intentional misdemeanor directly affecting the person, or when offender is resisting lawful arrest, in a manner not inherently dangerous.

Up to 21 years.

Louisiana Statutes Ann., Rev. 1950
§§ 14.30, 14.31

68

MAINE

Murder: Unlawfully killing human being with malice a-forethought, express or implied.

Life imprisonment.

Assault with intent to murder or kill if armed by dangerous weapon.

1 to 20 years.

Assault with intent to murder unarmed.

$1,000 or 10 years.

Attempted murder.

1 to 20 years.

Manslaughter: Unlawfully killing human being in heat of passion or sudden provocation, without express or implied malice aforethought, or being under legal duty to care and provide for child or any other person, willfully failing or neglecting to provide for such child or other person necessary food, clothing, treatment for sickness, etc. or causing or hastening death of such person, or committing manslaughter as defined by the common law.

$1,000 or 20 years.

Maine Rev. Statutes Anno., 17 §§ 2651-2657, 2551

MARYLAND

Murder--First Deg.: Perpetrated by means of poison, or lying in wait, or by any kind of willful, deliberate and premeditated killing; in perpetration of arson; in burning of any structure having tobacco, hay, horses, goods, etc.; in perpetration of rape, sodomy, mayhem, robbery, burglary or escape from Penitentiary.

Death or life imprisonment.

Second Deg.: All other murders.

Not more than 30 years.

Anno. Code of Maryland, 1957, 27 §§ 407-414

MASSACHUSETTS

Murder--First Deg: With deliberately premeditated

MASSACHUSETTS (continued)
malice aforethought or with extreme atrocity or cruelty, or in
the commission or attempted commission of a crime punishable
with death or imprisonment for life.

> Death or life imprisonment.
> Second Deg.: Other murders.
> Life imprisonment.
> Manslaughter: Not defined.
>> Up to 20 years, or up to $1,000 fine and impris-
>> onment up to 2 1/2 years.
>>> Ann. Laws of Massachusetts, Ch. 265,
>>> §§ 1, 2, 13

MICHIGAN
Murder--First Deg.: Perpetrated by means of poison, or
lying in wait, or any other kind of willful, deliberate and premeditated killing, or which shall be committed in the perpetration or
attempt to perpetrate any arson, rape, robbery or burglary.

> Life imprisonment.
> Second Deg.: All other kinds of murder.
> Life imprisonment or term of years.
> Manslaughter: Not defined.
>> Up to 15 years and/or up to $7,500.
>>> Compiled Laws of Michigan, 1948,
>>> §§ 750.316, 317, 321

MINNESOTA
Murder--First Deg.: When perpetrated with a premeditated design to effect the death of the person killed or of another.
> Life imprisonment.

Second Deg.: When committed with a design to effect the
death of the person killed or of another, but without deliberation
and premeditation, or when causing death while committing or
attempting to commit rape or sodomy with force or violence.
> Not more than 40 years.

Manslaughter--First Deg.: When intentionally causing
death in the heat of passion provoked by words or acts of another
that would provoke person of ordinary self-control under like cir-

70

MINNESOTA (continued)

cumstances; or causing death of another in committing or attempting to commit crime with such force and violence that death or
great bodily harm is reasonably foreseen and murder in first or
second degree was not committed thereby; or intentionally causing death of another because actor is coerced by threats and believes his act is only means of preventing his imminent death or
death to another.

Up to 15 years or $15,000 or both.

Second Deg.: Causing death by culpable negligence, shooting person believing him to be deer or other animal, setting
spring gun, pitfall, death fall, etc., or negligently knowingly
permitting dangerous animal to roam or confine it properly when
victim was not at fault.

Up to 7 years or $7,000 or both.

Minnesota Statutes Anno., §§ 609.18 to
609.205

MISSISSIPPI

Murder: When done with deliberate design to effect the
death of the person killed, or of any human being; when done in
commission of an act eminently dangerous to others, and evincing a depraved heart, regardless of human life, although without
any premeditated design to effect death; when done without any
design to effect death, by person engaged in commission or attempt to commit the crime of rape, burglary, arson, or robbery.

Death or life imprisonment.

Manslaughter: Killing while slayer was committing felony other than those specified for murder; killing while slayer
committing misdemeanor, where such killing would be murder
at common law; killing in heat of passion, without malice, but in
a cruel or unusual manner; killing in heat of passion, without
malice, by use of a dangerous weapon, without authority of law,
etc.

Not less than $500 and/or up to 20 years.

Mississippi Code Anno., 1942, §§ 2215,
2217, 2220, 2221, 2224, 2226,
2233

MISSOURI

Murder--First Deg.: Committed by means of poison, or by lying in wait, or by any other kind of willful, deliberate and premeditated killing, and every homicide in the perpetration or attempt to perpetrate any arson, rape, robbery, burglary, or mayhem.

Death or life imprisonment.

Second Deg.: All other kinds of murder except manslaughter or justifiable homicide.

Not less than 10 years.

Manslaughter: By act, procurement or culpable negligence of another, not murder or excusable or justifiable homicide.

$500 or more; or 6 mos. to 10 years; or $100 or more and not less than 3 months.

Vernon's Anno. Missouri Statutes,
559.010, 559.020, 559.030

MONTANA

Murder: Unlawful killing of a human being with malice aforethought.

First Deg: Perpetrated by means of poison, or lying in wait, torture, or by any other kind of willful, deliberate and premeditated killing, or which is committed in the perpetration or attempt to perpetrate arson, rape, robbery, burglary or mayhem, or perpetrated from a deliberate and premeditated design, unlawfully and maliciously, to effect the death of any human being other than him who is killed.

Death or life imprisonment.

Second Deg.: All other kinds of murder.

Not less than 10 years.

Manslaughter: Unlawful killing of a human being, without malice: Voluntary--upon a sudden quarrel or heat of passion; Involuntary--in the commission of an unlawful act, not amounting to felony; or in commission of lawful act which might produce death in an unlawful manner, or without due caution or circumspection.

Up to 10 years.

Rev. Codes of Montana, 1947,
§§ 94-2501, 94-2503, 94-2505,
94-2507, 95-2508

NEBRASKA

Murder--First Deg.: Purposely and of deliberate and premeditated malice, or in the perpetration of or attempt to perpetrate any rape, arson, robbery or burglary, or by administering poison, or causing the same to be done; or, by willful and corrupt perjury or subordination of the same, purposely procure the conviction and execution of any innocent person.

Death or life imprisonment.

Second Deg.: Purposely and maliciously, but without deliberation and premeditation.

10 years to life.

Manslaughter: Unlawfully kill, without malice, either upon a sudden quarrel, or unintentionally, while the slayer is in commission of some unlawful act.

1 to 10 years.

Rev. Statutes of Nebraska, 1943,
§§ 28-401 to 28-403

NEVADA

Murder: Unlawful killing of a human being, with malice aforethought, either express or implied.

First Deg.: Perpetrated by means of poison, or lying in wait, torture, or by any other kind of willful, deliberate and premeditated killing, or which shall be committed in the perpetration, or attempt to perpetrate, any arson, rape, robbery, or burglary, or committed by convict serving sentence of life imprisonment.

Death or life imprisonment.

Second Deg.: All other kinds of murder.

10 years to life.

Manslaughter: Unlawful killing, without malice express or implied, and without any mixture of deliberation. It must be voluntary, upon a sudden heat of passion caused by a provocation apparently sufficient to make the passion irresistible; or, involuntary, in the commission of an unlawful act, or a lawful act without due caution or circumspection.

Voluntary manslaughter
Up to 10 years.

NEVADA (continued)
> Involuntary manslaughter
>> 1 to 6 years and/or up to $5,000.
>> Nevada Compiled Laws, §§ 200.010 to
>> 200.090

NEW HAMPSHIRE

Murder--First Deg.: Committed by poison, starving, torture, or other deliberate and premeditated killing, or committed in perpetrating or attempting to perpetrate arson, kidnaping, rape, robbery or burglary.
> Death or life imprisonment.

Second Deg.: All other murder.
> Life imprisonment.

Manslaughter--First Deg.: Perpetrated with a design to effect death, or without such design by a person engaged in commission of any offense, or by person bearing any deadly weapon, open or concealed, or perpetrated in a cruel or unusual manner, or by means of deadly or dangerous instrument.
> Up to 30 years.

Second Deg.: By act, procurement or culpable negligence, which is not murder, nor manslaughter in first degree.
> Up to 10 years and/or up to $1,000.
>> New Hampshire Statutes Anno.,
>> § 2A: 113-1 to 113-5

NEW JERSEY

Murder--First Deg.: Killing a person by someone committing or attempting to commit arson, burglary, rape, robbery, sodomy or any unlawful act of which probable consequence may be bloodshed, or if death of anyone else results from such crime or act; killing any official in execution of his duty; killing private individual endeavoring to suppress an affray or to apprehend criminal.
> Death.

Second Deg.: Any other kind of murder.
> Imprisonment for not more than 30 years.

NEW JERSEY (continued)
Manslaughter: Not defined.
Not more than $1,000 or imprisonment for 10 years or both.
2A New Jersey Stats. Anno. §§ 113-114

NEW MEXICO
Murder: The unlawful killing of a human being, with malice aforethought, either express or implied.
First Deg.: Perpetrated by means of poison or lying in wait, torture, or by any kind of willful, deliberate and premeditated killing, or which is committed in the perpetration of or attempt to perpetrate any felony, or perpetrated from a deliberate and premeditated design unlawfully and maliciously to effect the death of any human being, or perpetrated by act greatly dangerous to lives of others, and indicating a depraved mind regardless of human life.
Death or life imprisonment.
Second Deg.: All other kinds of murder.
Not less than 3 years.
Manslaughter: Unlawful killing of a human being without malice. Voluntary: Upon a sudden quarren or in the heat of passion. Involuntary: In the commission of an unlawful act not amounting to felony, or in commission of lawful act which might produce death, in an unlawful manner or without due caution.
1 to 10 years.
New Mexico Statutes Anno., 40A-2-1 to 40A-2-3

NEW YORK
Murder: Acting with intent to cause the death of a person, and killing that person or a third person; or, engaging recklessly, under circumstances evincing depraved indifference to human life, in conduct which creates grave risk of death to another, and in fact does cause that death; or, acting alone or with others, commits or attempts to commit robbery, burglary, kidnaping, etc., and in the course of such crime he alone or any other participant, causes death of another, not a participant.
Life imprisonment.

75

NEW YORK (continued)

Manslaughter--First Deg.: Acting with intent to cause serious physical injury to another person, and causing death of such person or of a third person; or, with intent to cause the death of another person, causing death under circumstances which do not constitute murder because of acting under influence of extreme emotional disturbance, mitigating circumstances reducing murder to manslaughter first degree; or, committing abortional act which is justified pursuant to 125.05 section 3 prior to July 1, 1970, or intentionally causing or aiding another person to commit suicide.

Up to 15 years.

New York Penal Law, 125.10-125.25

NORTH CAROLINA

Murder--First Deg.: Perpetrated by means of poison, lying in wait, imprisonment, starving, torture or by any other kind of willful, deliberate and premeditated killing or killing committed in perpetration of, or attempt to perpetrate, arson, rape, robbery, burglary or other felony.

Death or life imprisonment.

Manslaughter: No definition.

4 mos. to 20 years.

Involuntary manslaughter.

Fine and/or imprisonment at discretion of Court.

General Statutes of North Carolina,

§§ 14-17 to 14-20

NORTH DAKOTA

Murder: Perpetrated without authority of law and with a premeditated design to effect the death of the person killed or of any other human being; when perpetrated by any act imminently dangerous to others and evincing a depraved mind, in disregard of human life, although without any premeditated design to effect the death of any particular individual; perpetrated without any design to effect death by a person engaged in commission of act or omission which may be punished by imprisonment in the Penitentiary.

76

NORTH DAKOTA (continued)

First Deg.: Perpetrated by means of poison, or by lying in wait, or by torture, or by other willful, deliberate, or premeditated killing or in committing or attempting to commit sodomy, rape, mayhem, arson, robbery or burglary.

Life imprisonment.

Second Deg.: All other kinds of murder.

10 to 30 years.

Manslaughter--First Deg.: Perpetrated without a design to effect death by a person while engaged in the commission of a misdemeanor; perpetrated without a design to effect death, and in a heat of passion, but in cruel and unusual manner or by means of a dangerous weapon; perpetrated unnecessarily either while resisting an attampt by the person killed to commit a crime, or after such attempt shall have failed.

5 to 15 years.

Second Deg.: Killing of one human being by the act, agency, procurement or culpable negligence of another.

Up to 5 years and/or up to $1,000.

North Dakota Rev. Code of 1943,
§§ 12-2708, 2712, 2713, 2714,
2717, 2718, 2719, 2720

OHIO

Murder--First Deg.: Purposely and either of deliberate and premeditated malice, or by means of poison, or in perpetrating or attempting to perpetrate rape, arson, robbery or burglary; maliciously places an obstruction on railroad, etc.

Death or life imprisonment.

Second Deg.: Purposely and maliciously kills another, except as provided for murder in first degree.

Life imprisonment.

Manslaughter--First Deg.: Unlawfully kills another (other than murder).

1 to 20 years.

Page's Ohio Rev. Code, 2901.01, 2901.5
to 2901.6

OKLAHOMA

Murder--Killing of one human being by another without authority of law, under the following circumstances: when perpetrated with premeditated design to effect death of person killed, or of any other human being; when perpetrated by any act imminently dangerous and evincing depraved mind regardless of human life, although without premeditated design to effect death of any individual; or when perpetrated without any design to effect death by a person engaged in the commission of a felony.

Death or life imprisonment.

Manslaughter--First Deg.: When perpetrated without design to effect death by person engaged in commission of misdemeanor; when perpetrated without design to effect death and in heat of passion, but in cruel or unusual manner or by means of dangerous weapon unless under circumstances that would be excusable or justifiable homicide; when perpetrated unnecessarily either when resisting attempt by person killed to commit crime or after such attempt shall have failed.

Not less than 4 years.

Second Deg.: Killing of one by gross or willful negligence.

2 to 4 years or imprisonment up to 1 year and/or $1,000 fine.

21 Oklahoma Statutes Annotated,
§§ 691, 701, 707, 711, 715-716

OREGON

Murder--First Deg.: Purposely, and of deliberate and premeditated malice, or in the commission or attempt to commit any rape, arson, robbery or burglary.

Life imprisonment.

Second Deg.: Purposely and maliciously, but without deliberation and premeditation, or in the commission or attempt to commit any felony, other than those listed above; killing by act imminently dangerous and evincing depravity.

Up to 25 years.

Manslaughter: Without malice express of implied, and without deliberation, upon a sudden heat of passion, caused by a provocation apparently sufficient to make the passion irresistible, voluntarily killing; in commission of unlawful act, or law-

OREGON (continued)

ful act without due caution or circumspection, involuntary killing, killing by act, procurement or culpable negligence (but not murder).

> 1 to 5 years and up to $5,000.
> Oregon Compiled Laws Anno.,
> 163.010-163.080

PENNSYLVANIA

Murder--First Deg.: Perpetrated by means of poison, or by lying in wait, or by any other kind of willful, deliberate and premeditated killing, or committed in perpetration of or attempt to perpetrate any arson, rape, robbery, burglary or kidnaping.

> Death or life imprisonment.

Second Deg.: All other kinds of murder.

> Up to 20 years and/or up to $10,000.

Manslaughter: Not defined.

Voluntary manslaughter--felony.

> Up to $6,000 and up to 12 years.

Involuntary manslaughter--happening in consequence of an unlawful act, or doing of lawful act in unlawful way.

> Up to $2,000 and/or up to 3 years.

> Purdon's Pennsylvania Statutes Anno.,
> Title 18, §§ 4701, 4703

RHODE ISLAND

Murder: Unlawful killing of a human being with malice aforethought.

First Deg.: Perpetrated by poison, lying in wait, or any other kind of willful, deliberate, malicious and premeditated killing, or committed in perpetration of or attempt to perpetrate any arson, rape, burglary or robbery, or while resisting arrest, or perpetrated from a premeditated design, unlawfully and maliciously to effect the death of any human being other than him who is killed.

> Life imprisonment.

Second Deg.: Any other murder.

> 10 years to life.

RHODE ISLAND (continued)
      Manslaughter: Not defined.
        Up to 20 years.
                General Laws of Rhode Island, 11-23-1
                   to 11-23-3

SOUTH CAROLINA

Murder: Killing of any person with malice aforethought, either express or implied.

        Death or life imprisonment.

Manslaughter: Unlawful killing of another without malice, express or implied.

        2 to 30 years.

Involuntary manslaughter.

        3 mos. to 3 years.

                Code of Laws of South Carolina, 1962,
                  §§ 16-51, 52, 55

SOUTH DAKOTA

Murder: When perpetrated with a premeditated design to effect the death of person killed or of any human being, perpetrated by act imminently dangerous to others and evincing a depraved mind, regardless of human life, although without any premeditated design to effect death of any individual; perpetrated without design to effect death by person committing felony; by act imminently dangerous to others evincing a depraved mind, regardless of human life.

        Life imprisonment or death.

Manslaughter--First Deg.: Perpetrated without design to effect death by person engaged in commission of misdemeanor involving moral turpitude, perpetrated without design to effect death and in heat of passion, but in cruel and unusual manner or by means of dangerous weapon; perpetrated unnecessarily either while resisting attempt by person killed to commit a crime or after such an attempt has failed.

        Not less than 4 years.

Second Deg.: Killing by act, procurement or culpable negligence which is not murder nor manslaughter in the first

SOUTH DAKOTA (continued)
degree.

> 2-10 years or 1 year and up to $1,000.
>> Compiled Laws, 1967, 22-16-1 to 22-16-29

TENNESSEE

Murder: Unlawfully kill any reasonable creature in being, and under the peace of the state, with malice aforethought, either express or implied.

First Deg.: Perpetrated by means of poison, lying in wait, or by any other kind of willful, deliberate, malicious and premeditated killing, or committed in the perpetration of or attempt to perpetrate, any murder in the first degree, arson, rape, robbery, burglary or larceny.

> Death or life or over 20 years.

Second Deg.: All other kinds of murder.

> 10 to 20 years.

Manslaughter: Unlawful killing of another without malice, either voluntary upon a sudden heat, or involuntary, but in the commission of some unlawful act.

> Voluntary manslaughter.
>> 2 to 10 years.

> Involuntary manslaughter.
>> 1 to 5 years.
>>> Tennessee Code Anno., 39-2401 to 39-2411

TEXAS

Murder: Voluntarily killing any person.

> Death or life or term of years not less than 2 years.

Manslaughter: Statute repealed. Homicide by negligence instead.

> First Deg.: In performance of a lawful act.
>> Up to 1 year or up to $1,000.

> In performance of an unlawful act which is misdemeanor.
>> Up to 3 years or up to $3,000.

TEXAS (continued)

In performance of unlawful act not offense against Penal Law.

Up to $1,000 and up to 1 year.

Vernon's Texas Penal Code, Arts. 1256-1257, 1230, 1237, 1242, 1243

UTAH

Murder: Unlawful killing of a human being with malice aforethought.

First Deg.: Perpetrated by poison, lying in wait or any other kind of willful, deliberate, malicious and premeditated killing; or committed in the perpetration of, or attempt to perpetrate, any arson, rape, burglary or robbery; or perpetrated from a premeditated design unlawfully and maliciously to effect the death of any human being other than one killed; or perpetrated by any act greatly dangerous to lives of others and evincing a depraved mind, regardless of human life.

Death or life imprisonment.

Second Deg.: Any other homicide as would be murder at common law.

10 years to life.

Manslaughter: Unlawful killing of a human being without malice.

Voluntary: Upon a sudden quarrel or in heat of passion.

1 to 10 years.

Involuntary: In commission of unlawful act not amounting to felony, or in commission of lawful act which might produce death, in unlawful manner or without due caution.

Up to 1 year.

Utah Code Anno., 1953, §§ 76-30.1 to 76-30.6

VERMONT

Murder--First Deg.: Murder committed by means of poison, lying in wait or by deliberate and premeditated killing, or committed in perpetrating or attempting to perpetrate arson, rape, robbery, or burglary.

Life imprisonment.

VERMONT (continued)

Murder of prison employee or law enforcement officer.
Death or life imprisonment as jury determines.
Second Deg.: Not defined.
Life or term as court shall order.
Manslaughter: Not defined.
Up to 15 years and/or $1,000.
Vermont Stats. Anno. 13, §§ 2301-2304

VIRGINIA

Murder--First Deg.: By poison, lying in wait, imprisonment, starving, or by any willful deliberate and premeditated killing, or killing in commission of, or attempt to commit, arson, rape, abduction, robbery or burglary.
Death or life imprisonment or not less than 20 years.
Second Deg.: All other murder.
5 to 20 years.
Manslaughter: Not defined.
Voluntary Manslaughter.
1 to 5 years or up to $1,000 and/or up to 1 year.
Code of Virginia, 1950, 18.1-21 to 18.1-25

WASHINGTON

Murder--First Deg.: With premeditated design to effect death of person killed, or another; by act imminently dangerous to others and evincing a depraved mind, regardless of human life, without premeditated design to effect death of any individual; or without design to effect death, by person in commission of or attempt to commit, or in withdrawing from the scene of, robbery, rape, burglary, larceny, or arson in first degree; or maliciously interfering or tampering with railroad.
Death or life imprisonment by special jury verdict.
Second Deg.: Committed with design to effect death, but without premeditation; perpetrated by person committing or attempting to commit, or withdrawing from scene of felony other than those enumerated for murder in the first degree.
Not less than 10 years.

WASHINGTON (continued)
Manslaughter: Other homicides, not excusable or justifiable.

> Up to 20 yrs. or up to 1 yr. and/or up to $1,000.
> Rev. Code of Washington Annotated,
> §§ 9.48.030, 9.48.040, 9.48.060

WEST VIRGINIA
Murder--First Deg.: By poison, lying in wait, imprisonment, starving, or by any willful, deliberate and premeditated killing, or in commission of, or attempt to commit, arson, rape, robbery, or burglary.

> Death or life imprisonment.

Second Deg.: All other murder.

> 5 to 18 years.

Manslaughter:

> Voluntary: 1 to 5 years.
> Involuntary: Up to 1 year and/or up to $1,000.
> West Virginia Code, 61-2-1 to 61-2-5.

WISCONSIN
Murder--First Deg.: Causing death with intent to do so.

> Life imprisonment.

Second Deg.: Causing death by act imminently dangerous to others, evincing depraved mind, regardless of human life.

> 5 to 25 years.

Third Deg.: Killing of human being without any design to effect death, by person engaged in commission of any felony.

> Up to 15 years more than the maximum penalty for the felony.

Manslaughter: Causing death by any one of the following: without intent to kill and while in the heat of passion; unnecessarily, in exercise of privilege of self-defense; coerced by threats which make person believe his act is only means of preventing death to himself or another; pressure of natural physical public disaster or imminent death to himself or another.

> Up to 10 years.
> West's Wisconsin Statutes Anno., 940.01-940.03, 940.05

WYOMING

Murder--First Deg.: With premeditated malice and purposely or in perpetration of, or attempt to perpetrate, rape, arson, robbery or burglary, or by poison.

Life imprisonment.

Second Deg.: Purposely and maliciously, but without premeditation.

20 years to life.

Manslaughter: Unlawfully kills without malice, express or implied, either voluntarily, upon sudden heat of passion, or involuntarily but in commission of unlawful act or by any culpable neglect or criminal carelessness.

Up to 20 years.

Wyoming Statutes, 1947, 6-54, 6-55, 6-58

Note: Code citations are current as of June 1, 1970, regardless of date of original volume.

Table No. 2

FIRST DEGREE MURDER PUNISHMENT

ALABAMA	Electrocution
ALASKA	Life imprisonment
ARIZONA	Gas
ARKANSAS	Electrocution
CALIFORNIA	Gas
COLORADO	Gas
CONNECTICUT	Electrocution
DELAWARE	Hanging
DISTRICT OF COLUMBIA	Electrocution
FLORIDA	Electrocution
GEORGIA	Electrocution
HAWAII	Life imprisonment
IDAHO	Hanging
ILLINOIS	Electrocution
INDIANA	Electrocution
IOWA	Life imprisonment
KANSAS	Hanging
KENTUCKY	Electrocution
LOUISIANA	Electrocution
MAINE	Life imprisonment
MARYLAND	Gas
MASSACHUSETTS	Electrocution
MICHIGAN	Life imprisonment
MINNESOTA	Life imprisonment
MISSISSIPPI	Gas
MISSOURI	Gas
MONTANA	Hanging
NEBRASKA	Electrocution
NEVADA	Gas
NEW HAMPSHIRE	Hanging

NEW JERSEY	Electrocution
NEW MEXICO	Life imprisonment
NEW YORK	Life imprisonment
NORTH CAROLINA	Gas
NORTH DAKOTA	Life imprisonment
OHIO	Electrocution
OKLAHOMA	Electrocution
OREGON	Life imprisonment
PENNSYLVANIA	Electrocution
RHODE ISLAND	Life imprisonment
SOUTH CAROLINA	Electrocution
SOUTH DAKOTA	Electrocution
TENNESSEE	Electrocution
TEXAS	Electrocution
UTAH	Hanging or shooting
VERMONT	Life imprisonment
VIRGINIA	Electrocution
WASHINGTON	Hanging
WEST VIRGINIA	Life imprisonment
WISCONSIN	Life imprisonment
WYOMING	Life imprisonment

BURGLARY AND ARSON, DEFINITIONS AND PENALTIES˙

ALABAMA

Burglary--First Deg.: In nighttime with intent to steal or commit felony, breaks and enters any inhabited dwelling or building.

Death or not less than 10 years.

Second Deg.: Daytime, breaks and enters inhabited dwelling; nighttime or daytime breaks and enters uninhabited dwelling or shop, store, etc., where goods are kept.

1 to 10 years.

Arson--First Deg.: Willfully or with intent to defraud sets fire or aids in burning of dwelling.

2 to 10 years (death or life imprisonment if death or maiming occurs).

Second Deg.: Burning of shops, store, etc., or other building or sets fire or aids burning of own property.

Code of Alabama, 14 §§ 23-31, 314-323

ALASKA

Burglary: Breaking and entering dwelling house with intent to commit crime, or armed with dangerous weapon breaks and enters, or assaults person lawfully therein.

1-10 years, unless at nighttime, up to 15 years.
If human being there, night or day, up to 20 years.
Not dwelling house, 2-5 years.

Breaking out of dwelling after committing, or attempting to commit crime.

1-3 years.

Arson--First Deg.: Willfully and maliciously setting fire to or burning or causing to be burned of aiding, counsel-

ALASKA (continued)

ling or procuring burning, of dwelling house, whether occupied, unoccupied or vacant, or part of or belonging to or adjoining dwelling, whether his property of that of another.

        2-20 years.

    Second Deg.: Building not described above.

        1-10 years.

    Third Deg.: Personal property of value of $100 or more.

        1-3 years and/or $3,000.

    Fourth Deg.: Attempted arson.

        1-2 years and/or $1,000.

    Defrauding insurer: 1-5 years and/or $5,000.

                Alaska Statutes, 11.20.010-11.20.130

ARIZONA

    Burglary: Entering building, house, office, etc., vessel, railroad car, motor vehicle, etc., with intent to commit grand or petit larceny or any felony.

    First Deg.: In nighttime

        1 to 15 years.

    Second Deg.: In daytime

        Up to 5 years.

    Arson--First Deg.: Sets fire, willfully and maliciously or aids burning of dwelling house, occupied or unoccupied, property of himself or another.

        2 to 20 years.

    Second Deg.: Burning any other property not included in first degree.

        1 to 10 years.

    Third Deg.: Burning of property of value of less than $25 and property of another.

        1 to 3 years.

    Fourth Deg.: Attempts to burn

        1 to 2 years or up to $1,000.

    Burning to defraud insurer

        1 to 5 years.

              Arizona Rev. Code, 13-231 to 13-236,
                  13-301 to 13-304

ARKANSAS

Burglary: Unlawfully entering house, tenement, railway car, automobile, airplane, or other building, boat, vessel, etc., with intent to commit a felony or larceny.

2 to 21 years.

Arson: Willfully and maliciously burn, or aids . . . in burning of any dwelling house, or other house, the property of himself or another.

1 to 10 years.

Arkansas Statutes, 1947, §§ 41-501,
41-1001, 41-1003

CALIFORNIA

Burglary: Enters any house, room, apartment, shop, warehouse, store, etc., or other building, vessel, railroad car, etc., with intent to commit grand or petit larceny or any other felony.

First Deg.: Burglary of inhabited dwelling or building in nighttime; either in day or night, by person armed with deadly weapon; in commission of burglary, assaults any person.

Not less than 5 years.

Second Deg.: All other kinds of burglary.

Up to 15 years.

Arson: Willfully and maliciously sets fire to or burns any dwelling house, property of himself or of another.

2 to 20 years.

Burning of building not dwelling house.

1 to 10 years.

California Penal Code, §§ 447a, 448, 459-61

COLORADO

Burglary--First Deg.: With intent to commit any felony, or steal property of any value, willfully and forcibly breaks or enters or willfully without force, enters humanly inhabited dwelling, building, railroad car or trailer, or enters with dangerous weapon, etc., or while entering, is within, or escaping therefrom, assaults any person.

5 to 20 years.

COLORADO (continued)

Second Deg.: Enters public or private building, railroad car or trailer, safe, cash register, coin box, telephone booth, etc., with intent to commit theft.

1 to 10 years.

Arson: First Deg.: Willfully and maliciously sets fire to or aids the burning of any dwelling, property of himself or another.

Up to 20 years.

Second Deg.: Burning of buildings other than dwellings.

Up to 10 years.

Third Deg.: Burning of personal property over $25 value.

Up to 3 years.

Burning to defraud: Up to 5 years.

Colorado Rev. Statutes, 1963, 40-3-1 to 40-3-8

CONNECTICUT

Burglary: with personal violence: Up to 25 years.

Attempted burglary: 10 years.

Possession of tools in night with intent to break and enter: Up to 5 years.

Burglary in daytime: Up to 4 years.

Breaking and entering without permission: Up to $500 or 1 year.

Breaking and entering with criminal intent: Up to 4 yrs.

Attempt to break and enter: 2 years; with force and violence 15 years.

Arson: Willfully and maliciously set fire to or burn or aid the burning of any vessel, dwelling house, church, whether the insured property of himself or of another.

2 to 20 years.

Burning of buildings other than dwellings.

6 months to 10 years.

General Statutes of Connecticut, 1958, 53-68, 75-79, 82-83

DELAWARE

Burglary--First Deg.: Breaking and entering in the night time dwelling of another with intent to commit murder or rape, whether such intent be executed or not.

25 to 40 years.

Second Deg.: At night time breaking and entering dwelling intending to commit crime other than murder or rape, whether executed or not; armed with dangerous weapon or assisted by confederate assaulting a person in commission of a crime.

5 to 20 years.

Third Deg.: Breaking and entering dwelling of another in circumstances not amounting to first or second degree burglary.

Up to 15 years.

Fourth Deg.: Entering building with intent, or committing crime, and breaking out.

Up to 5 years.

Arson--First Deg.: Willfully and maliciously burn or cause to be burned any dwelling, his own or that of another, in which there shall be at the time some human being, or any other building in which there shall be at the time some human being.

2 to 20 years.

Second Deg.: Where no human being is present.

$500 to $5,000 and 2 to 10 years.

Delaware Code Anno., 11-391 to 11-399

FLORIDA

Burglary: Breaks and enters a dwelling with intent to commit a felony, or after having entered breaks such a dwelling, if armed with dangerous weapon, or with dynamite, or if assaults any person lawfully therein.

Life imprisonment or term of years at court's discretion.

if not armed or with explosive

Up to 20 years.

Burglary of buildings other than dwelling, ship or vessel.

Up to 15 years.

Arson--First Deg.: Willfully and maliciously sets fire to or aids burning of any dwelling, occupied, unoccupied, or vacant property of himself or of another.

Up to 20 years.

FLORIDA (continued)

Second Deg.: Burning of any other building.

Up to 10 years.

Third Deg.: Burning of personal property of value of $25 or more

Up to 3 years.

Fourth Deg.: Attempts to burn

Up to 2 years or up to $1,000.

Florida Statutes Anno., §§ 806.01-806.07, 810.01-810.07

GEORGIA

Burglary: Breaking and entering into dwelling or any other building of another person, with intent to commit a felony or larceny.

1 to 20 years.

Arson: Knowingly damaging by fire or explosive dwelling of another without consent, occupied or unoccupied or vacant; building, watercraft, vehicle, etc., if designed for dwelling, or such building under circumstances where it is reasonably foreseeable that human life might be endangered.

1 to 20 years.

Second Deg.: Burning of any other building.

1 to 10 years.

Third Deg.: Burning of personal property of value of $25 or more

1 to 3 years.

Georgia Code Anno., §§ 26-2208 to 26-2211, 26-2401 to 26-2402

HAWAII

Burglary: Entering by night or day dwelling house, room, building, store, mill, vessel, with intent to commit larceny in first or second degree, or any felony.

First Deg.: Nighttime or any time when committed by one armed with deadly weapon or when place entered has occupant, without right to be there.

Up to 20 years.

HAWAII (continued)
>Second Deg.: All others.
>>Up to 10 years.
>Arson: Willfully and maliciously burning dwelling house of another.
>First Deg.: Burning at nighttime of occupied dwelling house.
>>Life imprisonment without parole, or life.
>Second Deg.: Burning in day or night dwelling house of another.
>>Life imprisonment or any number of years.
>>Hawaii Statutes, 723:1-4, 726:103

IDAHO
>Burglary: Entering any house, room, ship, warehouse, store, etc., or any other building, vessel, railroad car, etc., with intent to commit grand or petit larceny, or any felony.
>First Deg.: Burglary committed in the nighttime.
>>1 to 15 years.
>Second Deg.: Burglary committed in the daytime.
>>Up to 5 years.
>Arson--First Deg.: Willfully and maliciously setting fire to, aiding burning of any dwelling, occupied, unoccupied or vacant, property of self or another.
>>2 to 20 years.
>Second Deg.: Burning of building other than dwelling.
>>1 to 10 years.
>Third Deg.: Burning of personal property of value of $25 or more.
>>1 to 3 years.
>Fourth Deg.: Attempted burning.
>>1 to 2 years, or up to $1,000.
>>Idaho Code, 1947, 18-801-804, 18-1401-1404

ILLINOIS
>Burglary: Knowingly without authority entering or remaining without authority in a building, house, trailer, watercraft, aircraft, motor vehicle, with intent to commit felony or theft.
>>Indeterminate term not less than 1 year.

ILLINOIS (continued)

Arson: Damaging by fire or explosive real or personal property of value of $150 or more, of another, without his consent or with intent to defraud insurer.

Indeterminate term not less than 1 year.

Illinois Statutes Anno., 38, §§ 19-1 and 2;

§§ 20-1 and 2

INDIANA

Burglary--First Deg.: Breaks and enters into any dwelling with intent to commit any felony, or to do any act of violence or injury to any human being.

10 to 20 years.

Second Deg.: Buildings other than dwelling, boat, automobile, railroad car, etc., with intent to commit felony.

2 to 5 years.

Third Deg.: Any dwelling or other structure, with intent to commit misdemeanor; or enters land with intent to commit felony or sever crop or building, etc.

Up to $500 and/or up to 1 year.

Arson--First Deg.: Willfully and maliciously sets fire or aids the burning of any dwelling, occupied or unoccupied, property of another, or being insured sets fire for purpose of defrauding insurer.

2 to 14 years.

Second Deg.: Burning of any personal property, etc.

1 to 3 years.

Burns Indiana Statutes, 10-301, 10-304, 10-307

IOWA

Burglary: Break and enter dwelling house in nighttime with intent to commit any public offense; or, after entering, with such intent, break any dwelling in nighttime.

Armed burglary, or if assaults any person, or has confederate aiding in burglary

Life imprisonment or term of years

Otherwise than armed, etc.

Up to 20 years.

IOWA (continued)

Arson: Willfully and maliciously sets fire or aids burning of dwelling, property of himself or another.

Up to 20 years.

Burning of other buildings

Up to 10 years.

Iowa Code Anno., §§ 707.1 to 707.2

KANSAS

Burglary--First Deg.: Breaking and entering in nighttime, dwelling of another, where human being is then present, with intent to commit some felony, or some larceny, either by forcibly breaking wall, or outer door, window, or lock of door; or breaking in another manner, armed with dangerous weapon, or with assistance of confederate, or unlocking outer door with false keys, or picking lock, or breaking inner door.

10 to 21 years.

Second Deg.: Same as first, but in daytime; or circumstances at night where not first degree, breaking and entering, breaking to escape, breaking and entering in nighttime building other than dwellings, boats, railroad cars, etc.

5 to 10 years.

Third Deg.: Breaking and entering under circumstances which would have been second degree at nighttime.

Up to 5 years.

Arson--First Deg.: Burning of dwelling house, etc., property of another person.

2 to 20 years.

Second Deg.: Burning of building other than dwelling.

1 to 10 years.

Burning to defraud insurer.

1 to 5 years.

Fourth Deg.: Attempted burning.

6 months to 2 years, or up to $1,000.

Kansas Statutes, 1963, §§ 21-581 to 21-585,
21-513 to 21-518, 520, 521, 523

KENTUCKY
  Burglary: Not defined.
      2 to 20 years.
  Armed Assault with intent to rob.
      10 years or for life or death.
  Arson: Willfully and maliciously setting fire to or aiding
the burning of dwelling, property of himself or another.
      2 to 20 years.
  Burning of buildings other than dwellings.
      1 to 10 years.
  Burning of personal property.
      1 to 3 years.
  Attempted burning:
      1 to 2 years or $1,000.
            Baldwin's Kentucky Revised Statutes,
                  §§ 433.010, 433.020, 433.030,
                  443.040, 443.050, 433.120,
                  433.140

LOUISIANA
  Burglary--Aggravated: Unauthorized entering of any inhabited dwelling or any structure, water craft, or movable where
a person is present, with intent to commit a felony or any theft,
if armed with dangerous weapon, or committing battery upon any
person while in such place, or entering or leaving.
      1 to 30 years.
  Simple burglary: Not armed or without battery.
      Up to 9 years.
  Arson--Simple: Intentional damaging by any explosive substance or setting fire to any property of another, damage $500
or more.
            Up to $500 value, $1,000 and/or 1 year; over $500,
            $5,000 and/or 10 years.
  Aggravated: Intentional damaging by any explosive substance or setting fire to any structure, water craft, etc., where
it is foreseeable that human life might be endangered.
      2 to 20 years.
            Louisiana Statutes, Anno., Revised, R.S.
            14:51-14:53, 14:60, 14:62

97

MAINE

Burglary: Breaking and entering in nighttime with intent to commit felony or larceny, or, having entered with such intent, breaking in nighttime a dwelling house any person being then lawfully therein.

Imprisonment for any term of years.

Use of explosives to break and enter any building.

20 to 40 years.

Assault with intent to commit if armed with dangerous weapon.

1 to 20 years.

Not armed.

10 years or $1,000.

Breaking and entering with intent to commit same in daytime or entering without breaking at nighttime any building, any person there being put in fear.

10 years; if no person, 5 years or $500.

Arson--First Deg.: Willfully and maliciously setting fire to, burning, causing to be burned, or aiding burning of dwelling house, mobile home, house trailer, occupied, unoccupied, or vacant, whether property of self or another.

Up to 20 years.

Second Deg.: Any other building.

10 years and/or $5,000.

Third Deg.: Personal or real property of another.

3 years and/or $2,000.

Fourth Deg.: Attempted arson or preliminary act.

11 months and/or $1,000.

Burning to defraud insurance company.

Up to 5 years.

Maine Rev. Statutes Anno. 17:751-755, 151-157

MARYLAND

Burglary: Breaking and entering any dwelling in nighttime with intent to steal, take or carry away personal goods of another.

Up to 20 years, and restitution.

Breaking and entering in daytime, dwelling, with intent to commit felony, steal personal goods; or breaking storehouse,

MARYLAND (continued)

garage, etc., day or night, with intent to commit felony or steal goods of $100 or more.

Up to 10 years.

Arson: Burning of dwelling, property of himself or another.

Not more than 30 years.

Burning building other than dwelling.

Not more than 20 years.

Burning personal property of value of $25 or more.

Not more than 3 years.

Burning to defraud insurer.

5 years.

Attempted burning.

Not more than 2 years or up to $1,000.

Anno. Code of Maryland, Tit. 27, §§ 29-35

MASSACHUSETTS

Burglary: Break and enter in nighttime, dwelling, with intent to commit felony, or after entering, breaks such dwelling, any person being therein and armed with a dangerous weapon, or assaults person therein.

Life imprisonment or term not less than 10 years.

Break and enter in nighttime, dwelling, not armed, and no assault

5 years and up.

Break and enter building or ship in nighttime

Up to 20 years.

Entering dwelling in nighttime without breaking, or breaks and enters building or ship in daytime

Up to 10 years or up to 2 years and up to $500.

Arson: Burning dwelling house, property of himself or another, occupied or unoccupied.

Up to 20 years.

Burning of other buildings

Up to 10 years.

Annotated Laws of Massachusetts,
Ch. 266, §§ 1, 2, 14 to 18

MICHIGAN

Burglary: Breaking and entering, with intent to commit felony, or any larceny, any dwelling or other building.

Up to 15 years.

Burglary in daytime, entering without breaking.

Up to 5 years or up to $2,500.

Arson: Burning dwellinghouse, occupied, unoccupied, property of himself or another.

Up to 20 years.

Burning of other real property, other buildings.

Up to 10 years.

Burning of personal property, over $50 value.

Felony, penalty at discretion of court.

Burning of personal property, less than $50 value.

Fine or imprisonment, at discretion of court.

Burning with intent to defraud insurer.

Up to 10 years.

Compiled Laws of Michigan, §§ 750.72-
750.75, 750.110-750.111

MINNESOTA

Burglary--First Deg.: With intent to commit some crime, without consent, entering dwelling or related structure or banking business, with force or violence, either armed with dangerous weapon, or arming while therein with such weapon, or assisted by confederate actually present, or while engaged in effecting such entrance, committing any crime in building, assaulting any person therein.

Up to 20 years.

Second Deg.: With intent to commit crime, entering dwelling, etc., in which human being is present, under circumstances not amounting to first degree burglary.

Up to 10 years and/or $10,000.

Arson (aggravated arson): Destroying or damaging by fire or explosives his or another's property, real or personal, and creating danger to life or risk of bodily harm.

Up to 15 years and/or $15,000, if risk known.

Up to 5 years and/or $5,000, if risk not known but reasonably foreseeable.

MINNESOTA (continued)

Simple arson: Damaging or destroying property of another without his consent, if not aggravated arson.

Value of $100 or more, up to 3 years and/or $3,000.

Otherwise 90 days or $100 or both.

Minnesota Statutes Annotated, 609.56, 609.565, 609.58

MISSISSIPPI

Burglary: Breaking and entering, day or night, dwelling of another, in which there is some human being, with intent to commit some crime either by forcibly breaking wall, window, door, or other manner, or by assistance of confederate, or unlocking with false keys, or picking lock.

7 to 15 years.

Breaking and entering, in night, dwelling, armed, where human being is at time, with intent to commit some crime.

Up to 25 years.

Breaking and entering dwelling, day or night, with intent to commit some crime; breaking out of dwelling; breaking any door of dwelling at night, having entered; breaking inner door of dwelling by one lawfully in house.

Up to 10 years.

Breaking and entering building other than dwelling, in day or night.

Up to 7 years.

Arson--First Deg.: Willfully and maliciously sets fire or aids burning of dwelling, occupied, unoccupied or vacant, property of himself or another, or school (state-supported building).

2 to 20 years.

Second Deg.: Burning of property not included in first degree.

1 to 10 years.

Third Deg.: Burning of personal property of value of $25 and belonging to another.

1 to 3 years.

Fourth Deg.: Attempts to burn.

1 to 2 years or up to $1,000.

Burning of insured property.
1 to 5 years.
Mississippi Code Anno., 1942, §§ 2006-
2010, 2036-2043

MISSOURI

Burglary--First Deg.: Breaking and entering dwelling in which human being is present with intent to commit crime or steal, by forcibly breaking wall, window, lock; or breaking in any other manner, armed with dangerous weapon, or with assistance of confederate, then present; or unlocking outer door by false keys or picking lock.
5 to 20 years.

Second Deg.: Breaking and entering, with intent to commit crime or steal, under circumstances as are not burglary in first degree.
2 to 10 years.

Arson: Willfully sets fire or burns any dwelling, boat or vessel, etc., in which a human being is present, or bridge or causeway upon any railroad, property of himself or another.
Not less than 2 years.

Burning of shop, warehouse, factory, etc.
2 to 10 years.

Burning of other buildings, personal property of another; or burning of other buildings and personal property where he is owner with intent to injure or defraud; or burning of insured property; attempts to commit arson.
2 to 5 years.
Vernon's Anno. Missouri Statutes,
560.010-560.035, 560.040-560.135

MONTANA

Burglary: Enters any house, room, apartment, etc., shop, store, etc., or other building, automobile, vessel or railroad car, with intent to commit grand or petit larceny or any felony.
First Deg.: Committed in nighttime.
1 to 15 years.

MONTANA (continued)

Second Deg.: Committed in daytime.

Up to 5 years.

Arson--First Deg.: Willfully, feloniously and maliciously sets fire or aids the burning of any dwelling, occupied, unoccupied or vacant, property of himself or of another.

2 to 20 years.

Second Deg.: Burning of buildings other than dwellings.

1 to 10 years.

Third Deg.: Burning of personal property of value of $25
or more and property of another.

1 to 3 years.

Fourth Deg.: Attempts to burn.

Up to 6 months and/or up to $500.

Burning to defraud insurer.

1 to 5 years.

Revised Code of Montana, 1947, 94.501-
94.506, 94.901-94.903

NEBRASKA

Burglary: Breaks and enters dwelling, shop, office, etc.,
railroad car, etc., with intent to kill, rob, rape, or commit
any other felony, or with intent to steal property of any value.

1 to 10 years or up to $500.

In day or night, enters and attempts to kill, rob, steal,
rape or commit arson, or enters armed with dangerous weapon,
with intent to rob or steal and threaten to injure any person in
building or with intent to rob or order any person to hand over
money or property.

3 to 20 years.

Arson--First Deg.: Willfully and maliciously sets fire
or aids the burning of any dwelling, occupied, unoccupied or
vacant, property of himself or another.

2 to 20 years.

Second Deg.: Burning of other buildings or structure.

1 to 10 years.

Third Deg.: Burning of personal property, of value of $25
or more, and property of another.

1 to 3 years.

NEBRASKA (continued)
>Fourth Deg.: Attempts to burn.
>>1 to 2 years, or up to $1,000.
>Burning to defraud insurer.
>>1 to 5 years.

>>>Revised Statutes of Nebraska, 1943,
>>>§§ 28-504.1 to 28-504.5, 28-532,
>>>28-533

NEVADA

Burglary: Enters any house, room, apartment, etc., shop, warehouse, etc., or other building, vessel, railroad car, etc., with intent to commit grand or petit larceny, or any felony.

>1 to 10 years.

Arson--First Deg.: Willfully and maliciously sets fire or aids in the burning of dwelling, occupied or unoccupied or vacant, property of himself or another.

>2 to 20 years.

Second Deg.: Burning of other building.

>1 to 10 years.

Third Deg.: Burning of personal property, value of $25 or more and property of another.

>1 to 6 years.

Fourth Deg.: Attempted burning.

>>Up to one-half of longest term for offense attempted.

Burning to defraud insurer.

>1 to 6 years.

>>>Nevada Compiled Laws, 205.010-205.030,
>>>205.060

NEW HAMPSHIRE

Burglary: Entering building or occupied structure with purpose to commit crime therein.

>>If bodily harm is inflicted or attempted, or person is armed, $10,000 and/or 2-10 years.

All other: $5,000 and/or 1-5 years.

NEW HAMPSHIRE (continued)

Arson: Willfully and maliciously burn, or cause to be burned, dwelling house or outbuilding adjacent to it, or a part thereof.

Up to 30 years.

Personal property: Value of $25, up to 3 years or $1,000 and up to 1 year.

Insured property: Up to 5 years.

Attempted arson: Up to 2 years or $1,000.

New Hampshire Revised Statutes, 1955, 583A 1-3, 584.1, 584.5

NEW JERSEY

Burglary: Entering any church, dwelling, shop, vessel, or other building, etc., with intent to kill, rob, steal, commit rape, mayhem or battery.

Up to $2,000 and/or up to 7 years.

Arson: Willfully or maliciously burning or aiding burning of any dwelling, his own or another's.

Up to $2,000 and/or up to 15 years.

Burning ships and buildings other than dwellings.

Up to $2,000 and/or up to 7 years.

Burning to defraud insurer.

Up to $2,000 and/or up to 7 years.

New Jersey Statutes Anno., 2A 89-1, 94

NEW MEXICO

Burglary: Unauthorized entry of any vehicle, water craft, aircraft, dwelling or other structure with intent to commit any felony or theft therin.

1 to 5 years and up to $5,000.

Aggravated burglary: Unauthorized entry of any vehicle, water craft, aircraft, dwelling or other structure movable or immovable, with intent to commit felony or theft therein and person either is armed with deadly weapon or after entering arms self with one, commits battery upon person therein or while leaving.

10 to 50 years, and/or up to $10,000.

105

NEW MEXICO (continued)

Arson: Intentional damaging by any explosive substance or setting fire to any bridge, aircraft, water craft, vehicle, pipeline, utility line, communication line or structure, railway structure, private or public building, dwelling or other structure.

2 to 10 years, and/or up to $5,000.

Aggravated arson: Willful or malicious damaging by any explosive substance or willful or malicious setting fire to any bridge, aircraft, water craft, vehicle, pipeline, utility line, communication line or structure, railway structure, private or public building, dwelling or other structure, causing a person great bodily harm.

10 to 50 years and/or up to $10,000.

New Mexico Statutes, 40A-16-3, 16-4, 17-5, 17-6

NEW YORK

Burglary--First Deg.: With intent to commit crime, breaks and enters, in night, dwelling of another, in which there is at the time a human being, being armed with dangerous weapon, or arming inside with weapon, or assisted by confederate actually present, or while effecting entrance, or committing crime in building, or in escaping, assaults any person.

10 to 30 years.

Second Deg.: With intent to commit some crime, breaks and enters dwelling house in which there is human present, under circumstances not burglary in first degree.

Up to 15 years.

Third Deg.: With intent to commit crime, breaks and enters a building, being in any building, commits crime therein, and breaks out.

Up to 10 years.

Arson--First Deg.: Willfully burns in night, dwelling in which there is at the time a human being; or a car, etc., or other building, where to the knowledge of the offender, there is at the time, a human being.

Up to 40 years.

NEW YORK (continued)

Second Deg.: Commits an act of burning in daytime, which if at night, would be arson in first degree; willfully burns dwelling, in which no human being; willfully burns in nighttime, uninhabited building, but adjoining inhabited building, in which there is human, so as to endanger inhabited building; wilfully burns in night, car, etc., or other building, ordinarily occupied in night by human, although no person within at the time, willfully burns car, etc., or other building, which is insured.

Up to 25 years.

Third Deg.: Burns personal property of another of value of $25 or over.

New York Penal Law (McKinney, 1967),
Art. 140, 150

NORTH CAROLINA

Burglary--First Deg.: If committed in dwelling house, and any person is in actual occupation of part of house at time of burglary.

Death or life imprisonment.

Second Deg.: Committed in dwelling house, not actually occupied by anyone at time of crime.

Life imprisonment or term of years.

Arson: Not defined.

Death or life imprisonment.

Schools, public buildings.

5-10 years.

Attempted arson.

4 mos.-10 years.

Punishment for other types of burning, for example, churches, etc.

20 to 40 years.

General Statutes of North Carolina,
§§ 14-51 to 14-67

NORTH DAKOTA

Burglary: Breaking into dwelling house by forcibly breaking wall or outer door, window, etc.; breaking in dwelling house in any manner with intent to commit a crime; breaking into dwelling armed with dangerous weapon or assisted by confederate actually present; breaking into dwelling by unlocking outer door with false keys or picking lock; entering dwelling in nighttime through open door, window, etc., and breaking inner door, window, etc., with intent to commit a crime; being lawfully in dwelling, in nighttime, breaking inner door with intent to commit crime; in nighttime breaking door, window, etc., in order to get out after having committed crime in dwelling, breaking and entering at any time any building, tent, railroad car, motor vehicle, vessel, etc., with intent to steal or commit felony.

1 to 10 years.

Arson: Willfully and maliciously setting fire to, aiding burning of any dwelling house, property of himself or of another.

2 to 20 years.

Arson of buildings other than dwellings.

1 to 10 years.

Arson to personal property over value of $25, and property of another.

1 to 3 years.

Arson of insured personal property.

1 to 5 years.

Attempted arson.

1 to 2 years, or up to $1,000.

North Dakota Century Code, §§ 12-34-01, 12-34-06, 12-35-02

OHIO

Burglary: In night season, maliciously and forcibly breaking and entering an inhabited dwelling house with intent to commit a felony or with intent to steal property of any value.

Life or 5 to 30 years.

Burglary in an uninhabited dwelling or other building.

1 to 15 years.

Arson: Willfully and maliciously or with intent to defraud, setting fire or aiding burning of any dwelling, property of himself or another, or any inhabited structure or building.

2 to 20 years.

OHIO (continued)
Burning of other buildings or bridge.
1 to 10 years.
Burning personal property with intent to defraud insurer.
1 to 5 years.
Burning personal property of another, of value of $25.
1 to 3 years.
Attempted burning.
1 to 2 years, or up to $1,000.
Page's Ohio Rev. Code Anno., 2907.02-2907.10

OKLAHOMA
Burglary--First Deg.: Breaking and entering in the nighttime the dwelling house of another, in which there is at the time some human being, with intent to commit some crime, either by forcibly breaking wall, outer door, window, etc.; by breaking in in some other manner, being armed with dangerous weapon or assisted by confederate actually present; or by unlocking an outer door by false keys or picking lock, or opening a window.
7 to 20 years.
Second Deg.: Breaking and entering building or any part of any building, room, booth, tent, railroad car, automobile, truck, trailer, vessel, or other structure or erection, in which any property is kept; breaking into or forcibly opening any coin operated or vending machine or device with intent to steal any property therein or to commit any felony.
2 to 7 years.
Arson--First Deg.: Willfully and maliciously setting fire to or burning or destroying in whole or in part, by the use of any explosive device or substance, causing to be burned or destroyed, or aiding, counselling, procuring, burning or destruction of any dwelling house or adjoining outhouse or garage or contents thereof, whether occupied, unoccupied, or vacant, the property of himself or another.
Up to 20 years and/or up to $25,000.
Second Deg.: Willful and malicious burning of any building or structure, public or private, other than dwelling houses or contents thereof, property of himself or another.
Up to 15 years and/or up to $20,000.

OKLAHOMA (continued)

Third Deg.: Willful and malicious burning of personal property, automobiles, etc., standing farm crops, etc., of value of $20, property of himself or another.

Up to 5 years and/or $5,000.

Fourth Deg.: Attempted burning of property mentioned in foregoing.

Up to 3 years and/or $2,000.

Oklahoma Statutes Anno., 21 §§ 1401-1404; 1431, 1435-1441

OREGON

Burglary: Breaking and entering dwelling containing human being, with intent to commit crime, or having entered with such intent, breaking in nighttime a dwelling house, or armed with dangerous weapon or assaults person.

Up to 15 years.

Breaking and entering building, railroad car, vessel, etc.

Up to 10 years.

Breaking to get out of dwelling house, in nighttime, after committing or attempting to commit crime.

Up to 3 years.

Arson--First Deg.: Willfully and maliciously setting fire or aiding burning of dwelling house, any building part of dwelling house, etc., any public building in which there is at the time a human being.

20 years.

Second Deg.: Burning of building not in first degree category.

10 years.

Third Deg.: Burning of other property, being property of another.

Up to 1 year.

Attempted burning.

Up to 3 years and/or up to $1,000.

Oregon Rev. Statutes, 164.010, 164.230, 164.240, 164.250

PENNSYLVANIA

Burglary: At any time, willfully and maliciously, enters any building, with intent to commit any felony.

Up to $10,000 and/or up to 20 years.

Arson: Willfully and maliciously, sets fire or aids the burning of any dwelling house, property of himself or another.

Up to 20 years and/or up to $10,000.

Burning, etc., of any other building or structure.

Up to 10 years and/or up to $5,000.

Burning of personal property to defraud insurer.

Up to 7 years and/or up to $3,000.

Burning of personal property of another, of value of $25.

Up to 2 years and/or up to $1,000.

Attempts to commit arson.

Up to 2 years and/or up to $1,000.

Purdon's Pennsylvania Statutes, Ann.,
Title 18, §§ 4901, 4905-4908

RHODE ISLAND

Burglary: (not defined)

Life or term not less than 5 years.

Breaking and entering any bank, shop, etc., public building, vessel, in nighttime with intent to commit murder, rape, robbery or larceny.

Up to 10 years.

Break and enter at day or night any dwelling house, occupied or not.

Up to 3 years and/or up to $300.

Enter any dwelling day or night, with intent to commit murder, rape, robbery, arson or larceny; or with such intent, during the day, enter any other building, ship or vessel.

Up to 10 years and/or up to $500.

Arson: (not defined)

1 year to life.

Wrongfully or maliciously sets fire or aids the burning of any dwelling, or dynamites, etc., the burning whereof is not arson at common law.

2 to 20 years.

RHODE ISLAND (continued)

Burning, etc., of personal property of another of value of $25.

1 to 3 years.

Burning of personal property to defraud insurer

1 to 5 years.

Attempts to burn or dynamite

Up to $1,000 and/or 1 to 2 years.

General Laws of Rhode Island, 11-4-1 to
11-4-6, 11-8-1 to 11-8-5

SOUTH CAROLINA

Burglary: As at common law.

Life or 5 years and up.

Break and enter, or break with intent to enter, in daytime, dwelling house, or in nighttime, with intent to commit felony or other crime of lesser grade.

Up to 5 years.

Arson: Willfully and maliciously sets fire to or aids the burning of any dwelling, property of himself or another.

2 to 20 years.

Burning of other buildings

1 to 10 years.

Burning of personal property to defraud insurer

1 to 5 years.

Burning of personal property

1 to 3 years.

Code of Laws of South Carolina, 1952,
§§ 16-311 to 16-314, 16-331,
16-332

SOUTH DAKOTA

Burglary--First Deg.: Breaks into and enters in nighttime dwelling of another, in which human being is at time present, with intent to commit crime therein, by forcibly breaking wall or door or window, etc., breaking in any other manner being armed with dangerous weapon or aided by confederate actually present or by unlocking door with false keys or picking lock.

Not less than 10 years.

SOUTH DAKOTA (continued)

Second Deg.: Breaking into dwelling house in daytime un der such circumstances as would have been burglary in first de gree if at night; entered dwelling in nighttime through open doo or window and breaking any inner door or window, etc., with in tent to commit any crime; lawfully in dwelling house and breakin in nighttime inner door with intent to commit any crime, an building, inhabited or not and opening or attempting to open, safe vault, etc., by using explosives.

     5 to 15 years.

Third Deg.: Breaking into dwelling house in nighttime with intent to commit a crime, but not first degree burglary breaking or entering at any time any other building, railroad car vessel, etc., with intent to commit larceny or any felony.

     Up to 15 years.

Fourth Deg.: Breaks and enters dwelling house, with in tent to commit crime, where not burglary in any other degree or having committed crime in dwelling, breaks in nighttime oute door or window, etc., to get out.

     Up to 3 years.

Arson: Willfully sets fire to or aids the burning of an dwelling, property of himself or another.

     Up to 20 years.

Arson of building other than dwelling, property of himse or another.

     Up to 10 years.

Arson of personal property, property of another and ($25 value.

     Up to 3 years.

Arson of insured personal property.

     Up to 5 years.

Attempted arson.

     Up to 2 years, or up to $1,000.

          South Dakota Compiled Laws, 1967,
                    22-33-1 to 22-33-7, 22-32-1 ।
                    22-32-16

TENNESSEE

Burglary: Breaking and entering dwelling house by nigh

with intent to commit felony.

> 5 to 15 years.

Second Deg.: Breaking or entering by day, with intent to commit felony.

> 3 to 15 years.

Third Deg.: Breaking and entering business house or building other than dwelling, with intent to commit felony.

> 3 to 10 years.

Breaking and entering freight or passenger car, motor vehicle, by day or night, with intent to steal anything of value or commit felony.

> 3 to 10 years.

Arson: Willfully and maliciously setting fire to or aiding burning of any house or building, property of himself or another.

> 3 to 21 years.

Burning bridge, railroad, vehicle, aircraft, etc.

> 1 to 10 years.

Burning personal property, property of himself of another, of value of $25 or more.

> 1 to 10 years.

Attempted arson.

> 1 to 5 years.

> Tennessee Code Anno., 39-501 to 39-509

TEXAS

Burglary: Entering house by force, threats or fraud, at night or in like manner entering either day or night and remaining concealed therein, with intent to commit felony or crime of theft.

> 2 to 12 years.

Breaking and entering in daytime, with intent to commit felony or theft.

> 2 to 12 years.

Burglary of private residence at night.

> Not less than 5 years.

Attempted burglary.

> 2 to 4 years.

Arson: Willfully burning any house (owner liable for

TEXAS (continued)

burning own house, when it is within town or city, or is insured, or within which is property of another, or where there is apparent danger to life of person or danger to some other house.)

2 to 20 years.

Burning of other buildings.

2 to 5 years or up to $2,000.

Burning of insured personal property.

2 to 5 years.

Attempted arson.

1 to 7 years.

Vernon's Texas Penal Code, Arts. 1304, 1312, 1314, 1316, 1318, 1322, 1389 to 1391, 1397 to 1402

UTAH

Burglary--First Deg.: Forcibly breaking and entering or entering with force open window, door, of any house or building, or vessel, etc., with intent to commit larceny or any felony by use of dynamite, firearms, etc.

25 to 40 years.

Second Deg.: Forcibly breaking and entering, or without force entering open door, window, etc, of house or other building, or vessel, etc., with intent to commit larceny or any felony.

1 to 20 years.

Third Deg.: In daytime entering dwelling house or other building or vessel, etc., with intent to steal or commit any felony.

6 months to 3 years.

Arson--First Deg.: Willfully and maliciously setting fire to or aiding burning of any dwelling house, property of himself or another.

2 to 20 years.

Second Deg.: Burning of other buildings.

1 to 10 years.

Third Deg.: Burning of personal property of another, of value of not less than $25.

1 to 3 years.

115

UTAH (continued)
> Burning of insured personal property.
>> 1 to 5 years.
> Attempted burning.
>> 1 to 2 years or up to $1,000.
>>> Utah Code Anno., 1953, §§ 76-6.1 to
>>> 76-6.5, 76-9.1 to 76-9.6

VERMONT
> Burglary: In nighttime, breaking and entering dwelling, bank, shop, store, etc., vessel, railroad car, or other building in which personal property is situated, with intent to commit murder, rape, robbery, larceny or other felony.
>> Up to 15 years and/or up to $1,000.
> Burglary as above, but in daytime.
>> Up to 10 years or up to $1,000.
> Arson--First Deg.: Willfully and maliciously setting fire to or aiding burning of dwelling house, occupied, unoccupied or vacant, property of himself or another.
>> 2 to 10 years or up to $2,000.
> Death resulting--murder first degree.
> Second Deg.: Burning of other buildings or structures, property of himself or another.
>> 1 to 5 years or up to $1,000.
> Third Deg.: Burning of personal property not less than $25 value, and property of another.
>> 1 to 3 years or up to $500.
> Fourth Deg.: Attempted arson.
>> 1 to 2 years or up to $500.
>>> Vermont Statutes Anno., 13-1201 to
>>> 13-1202, 13-501 to 13-509

VIRGINIA
> Burglary: Breaking and entering dwelling of another in nighttime with intent to cimmit felony or larceny, even though thing stolen is less than $50 value.
>> Death or life, or not less than 5 years.
> In night without breaking, or in daytime breaking and en-

tering dwelling occupied, or office, shop, etc., railroad car, automobile (if used as dwelling place) etc., with intent to commit murder, rape, or robbery.

1 to 20 years.

As above, but with intent to commit larceny or other felony.

1 to 20 years, or up to 12 months and up to $1,000.

As above, but with intent to commit assault or other misdemeanor.

1 to 10 years, or up to 1 year $1,000.

Arson: In nighttime, maliciously burning or using explosive, or aiding burning of any dwelling, property of himself or another.

Death or 5 to 20 years.

If occupied, but in daytime; or barn at night, meeting house, college, etc.

3 to 15 years; unoccupied 2 to 10 years.

Burning of personal property, of value of $100 or more.

3 to 10 years.

Burning of personal property, of value of less than $100.

2 to 5 years.

Burning of other buildings, if no one present and property of value of $100 or more.

2 to 10 years.

If no one present and property of less than $100 value.

1 to 5 years.

Threats--1 to 10 years or up to 1 year and $1,000.

Burning to defraud insurer.

1 to 10 years.

Code of Virginia, 18.1-75 to 18.1-85,
18.1-86 to 18.1-89

WASHINGTON

Burglary--First Deg.: With intent to commit some crime, enters in nighttime, dwelling of another in which at the time a human being is present, armed with dangerous weapon, or arming inside with weapon, or assisted by confederate actually present, or while making entrance or in committing crime therein or es-

117

sisted by confederate actually present, or while making entrance or in committing crime therein or escaping, assaults any person; with intent to commit crime, breaks and enters bank, post office, railway express, etc.

Not less than 5 years.

Second Deg.: With intent to commit crime, where not burglary first degree, breaks and enters, or enters dwelling house, or having committed crime breaks out of any building where property is kept.

Up to 15 years.

Arson--First Deg.: Willfully burns in nighttime dwelling of another, or any building in which there is at the time a human being; sets fire dangerous to any human life.

Not less than 5 years.

Second Deg.: Willfully burns any building, automobile, bridge, etc., or other property.

Up to 10 years and/or up to $5,000.

Rev. Code of Washington, 1951, §§ 9.09.010, 9.10.010, 9.19.020

WEST VIRGINIA

Burglary: In nighttime, break and enter, or enter without breaking, or in daytime break and enter, dwelling, with intent to commit felony or larceny.

1 to 15 years.

In daytime, enter without breaking a dwelling, with intent to commit felony or any larceny.

1 to 10 years.

Break and enter, or enter, building other than dwelling.

1 to 10 years.

Break and enter, or enter, automobile, etc.

2 to 12 months and up to $100.

Arson--First Deg.: Willfully and maliciously sets fire to or aids the burning of dwelling, occupied, unoccupied or vacant, property of himself or another.

2 to 20 years.

Second Deg.: Burning of other building or structure

1 to 10 years.

WEST VIRGINIA (continued)
 Third Deg.: Burning of personal property of another of
$50 value
                1 to 3 years.
        Fourth Deg.: Attempts to commit arson
                1 to 2 years or up to $1,000.
        Burning insured property
                1 to 5 years.
                        West Virginia Code, 61-3-1 to 61-3-5,
                                61-3-12

WISCONSIN
        Burglary: Breaking and entering without consent, with in-
tent to commit felony, any building, dwelling, railroad car, ship,
etc.
                Up to 10 years.
        If with dangerous weapon, explosive, battery on person
therein.
                Up to 20 years.
        Arson: By fire intentionally damaging building of another
without his consent; doing so with intent to defraud insurer; or
doing so by means of explosives.
                Up to 15 years.
        Destroying property other than building, value of $100 or
more.
                $1,000 and/or up to 3 years.
        Damaging property other than building with intent to defraud.
                $1,000 and/or up to 5 years.
                        West's Wisconsin Statutes Anno., 943.02-
                                943.04, 943.10

WYOMING
        Burglary: Breaking and entering dwelling house, shop, of-
fice, warehouse, etc., or buildings, with intent to commit felony
or steal property of any value.
                Up to 14 years.
        If armed with dangerous weapon, or using explosives or
committing battery.
                5 to 50 years.

WYOMING (continued)

Arson--First Deg.: Willfully and maliciously setting fire or aiding burning of any dwelling, occupied or vacant, property of himself or another.

2 to 20 years.

Second Deg.: Burning of any other building or structure, property of himself or another.

1 to 10 years.

Third Deg.: Burning of personal property, of value of $25 and property of another.

1 to 3 years.

Wyoming Statutes, 1957, 6-121 to 6-125,
6-129 to 6-130

Note: Code citations are current as of June 1, 1970, regardless of date of original volume.

INDEX